IT'S A
PLEASURE

VIRPI MIKKONEN

IT'S A
PLEASURE

**SWEET TREATS WITHOUT GLUTEN,
DAIRY, AND REFINED SUGAR**

weldon**owen**

CONTENTS

THIS BOOK IS DEDICATED TO ALVA & FINN,
TWO OF THE SWEETEST PEOPLE IN MY LIFE.

INTRODUCTION

This book is dedicated to all the foodies and dessert lovers out there—to people who wish to enjoy pure and clean sweets and who want to feel good after indulging. My aim is to bring fresh ideas and inspiration for creating cakes, cookies, ice cream, and confections by offering new delicious and healthy options.

In my opinion, true indulgence means that after eating a dessert you still feel good and fresh and have no guilt over what you've enjoyed. That is why I've replaced low-quality ingredients with wholesome and fresh ones. I've stripped my recipes of all ingredients that might cause you to feel unwell, and spooned in ones that will make you feel good. Sweet treats do not need to be vices; they can also be virtues!

In my recipes I respect natural flavors and nutritious raw ingredients, and blissfully ignore white sugar and wheat. I feel that these cause more harm than good and leave you feeling worse off. And there's no need for them. There are tastier alternatives for both when it comes to baking.

Organic and unprocessed ingredients are at the heart of my recipes. I wish to create simple and easy desserts that tempt more experienced bakers as well. To preserve the good in the ingredients, half of the recipes in this book require no heating. All the recipes in the book are free of gluten, dairy, and yeast. A large portion of the recipes are grain-free and vegan, or at least can be prepared without animal products, so that as many people as possible can find and create their own favorite treats.

All the recipes and images are my own handiwork. Each treat has been baked with love, and I've tested my favorites many times over! I hope that my book encourages you to respect your body, to offer it only the best-quality food—and above all, to enjoy and savor desserts with no guilt!

Become a dessert foodie of the new era, and surrender to pure pleasure!

♥ *Virpi*

ABOUT THE INGREDIENTS

All the ingredients are available from well-stocked grocery stores and natural-foods shops, and many can be found online. In some cases, they can be made at home.

FLOURS & EXTRACTS

ALMOND FLOUR. This high-fiber, flavorsome flour is one of my favorites. Almond flour, like many gluten-free flours, does not create the structure that certain doughs need to rise and hold firmly together. To achieve this, you will need to use baking powder combined with psyllium powder to create the bind. You can also find coarser almond meal made of raw almonds. Be mindful that coarser almond meal usually absorbs less liquid than finely ground almond flour, because it contains more fat.

COCONUT FLOUR. Naturally sweet coconut flour is my other favorite. It's used like almond flour, or with it. Coconut flour absorbs liquid from other ingredients, so you usually need about one-third the amount of normal flour.

NUT FLOURS. Different nut flours can replace a portion of any flour, creating new nuances in taste. People allergic to nuts can try seed flours, like pumpkin seed flour. You can make your own nut flour by grinding the nuts with a high-speed blender. Make sure not to overgrind, to prevent the flour from turning into nut butter—mind you, though, that is also a great baking ingredient!

OAT FLOUR. Gluten-free oat flour can be made at home by grinding gluten-free oats in a high-speed blender. Oat flour creates great structure, but dough made from it can easily turn pastelike. Combine with other flours, such as psyllium husk powder or xanthan gum.

PSYLLIUM HUSK POWDER. Created from the seeds of the plantain plant, this powder soaks up liquid. It's used to add structure and fluffiness to gluten-free baking. It also makes handling dough easier.

TAPIOCA FLOUR. Mild-tasting tapioca flour is made from a tropical root called cassava. You can use it to add moisture and texture to pastries, or as a thickening agent.

XANTHAN GUM. Made by fermenting sugar in liquid, this powder gives nice texture and structure. It's best mixed with flour when creating cakes and cookies.

GROUND FLAXSEEDS & CHIA SEEDS. Both flaxseeds and chia seeds create a gel when combined with water. The gel can be used to create structure in baking. Use ground flaxseeds or grind the seeds in a spice grinder. Whisk 1 tablespoon of the ground flaxseeds and 3 tablespoons of water together. Let the mixture sit in the fridge for 15 minutes. The mixture is also called a "flaxseed egg," and it can replace eggs in many recipes.

SWEETENERS

DRIED FRUITS. Fresh dates as well as dried organic dates, figs, apricots, and raisins are great for baking as long as they were processed without sulfur oxide. Rich in nutrients, they add a lovely color and flavor to sweets when puréed. They're digested more easily when soaked. You can also try using puréed fresh fruits as a sweetener.

HONEY. Delicate-tasting honey is a great sweetener for all cooking. Honey retains most of its valuable nutrients if it has not been heated or pasteurized. I favor locally sourced organic honey to support local bees and farmers. Vegans can substitute honey with coconut palm syrup or maple syrup.

STEVIA. Extracted from the stevia plant, this sweetener comes in powder and liquid forms. It contains no sugar and does not raise blood glucose levels. The taste can be strong, so use in moderation, preferably with other sweeteners. Always choose organic.

COCONUT BUTTER. Naturally sweet coconut butter can replace both fat and sweetener in a recipe, partly or completely. Coconut butter is easy to make at home (see page 126).

COCONUT (PALM) SUGAR & SYRUP. The sugar made by tapping the sweet nectar from the tropical coconut palm tree flower is caramel-like and full of flavor. It has a low glycemic index, so it doesn't cause blood sugar levels to fluctuate as white sugar does. Use like regular sugar or syrup. Vegans can replace honey with coconut syrup.

BANANA POWDER, LUCUMA, LUO HAN GUO POWDER, & XYLITOL. Additional options; find online.

CACAO & COCONUT

CACAO BUTTER. Cold-pressed cacao butter, extracted from cacao beans at low temperatures, is the best in quality. To make sure your chocolate keeps well at room temperature, use cacao butter as the sole fat. Cacao butter melts into liquid at 95°F.

CACAO NIBS. Cacao nibs, pieces of peeled and crushed cacao bean, can be used in or on top of chocolate to give it a crunchy texture. Nibs contain all of the health benefits of cacao—raw nibs contain magnesium, iron, zinc, manganese, copper, chromium, and several group B vitamins. In addition, cacao includes the mood-improving hormone serotonin and abundant antioxidants.

RAW CACAO PASTE. Cacao paste is made of peeled and ground cacao beans. It's a great ingredient for making chocolate. It is solid at room temperature and liquid at 122°–140°F.

RAW CACAO POWDER. Along with cacao butter, cacao powder is a basic ingredient in chocolate making. Cacao powder is made when fat is extracted from cacao paste. Quality cacao powder is produced at temperatures under 113°F, preserving the nutrients. Tip! If you are sensitive to cacao, try replacing cacao powder partly or completely with chocolate-tasting carob powder.

COCONUT OIL. I love using coconut oil in many of my recipes because it suits baking wonderfully. I prefer cold-pressed virgin coconut oil. It is made by pressing the oil out of dried ground white nutmeat, with temperatures kept low so that the oil preserves its health benefits.

CHOCOLATES
&
CONFECTIONS

BASIC CHOCOLATE

MAKES ABOUT ½ CUP (4 OZ)

½ cup grated cacao butter
5 tablespoons coconut oil
½ cup raw cacao powder
¼ cup honey or coconut syrup
Pinch of sea salt

Melt the cacao butter and coconut oil until smooth in the top of a double boiler. Add the cacao powder, honey, and salt and mix. Taste and adjust the sweetness if necessary. Use melted as a topping or icing, or pour the chocolate into silicone chocolate-bar molds and freeze for about 15 minutes.

Raw chocolate is chocolate that has not been heated to over 118°F. This preserves the enzymes and nutrients of the chocolate. The quality of your ingredients is important, so aim to use organic and top-shelf brands. You can taste the quality immediately in chocolate as well as feel it in the consistency. Good-quality cacao products have been manufactured as gently as possible, keeping the nutrients intact.

By tempering the raw chocolate you can create a desirable, melt-in-your-mouth chocolate-bar consistency that snaps when you break the chocolate. Tempering is also called "pre-crystallizing" chocolate, and will also keep the chocolate from melting at room temperature. Warm the chocolate to 118°–120°F in the top of a double boiler, using a candy thermometer to monitor the temperature. Stir with a spoon. Place the double boiler top (or bowl) with the chocolate over a container of cold water to cool the chocolate to 79°–81°F. Last, reheat the chocolate again to 88°–90°F. Pour into molds or onto a dish and freeze.

This chocolate makes a great base for flavored chocolates and can also be used as an icing for chocolate candy or truffles.

CHOCOLATE BANANA BITES

MAKES ABOUT 24 PIECES

2 ripe bananas
½ cup raw cacao paste
2 tablespoons honey
1 teaspoon vanilla
    extract
Pinch of sea salt

ON TOP
Coconut flakes

Peel and chop the bananas into pieces about ¾ inch long. Place the pieces in a dish and place in the freezer while you prepare the chocolate icing.

Grate the cacao paste into a heat-resistant bowl and melt in the top of a double boiler. Add the honey, vanilla extract, and salt and stir into an even mixture. Dip the frozen banana pieces into the melted chocolate. The chocolate will quickly set over the cold banana. Sprinkle with coconut flakes and return to the freezer for another 30 minutes. Bring the banana bites to room temperature, serve, and enjoy. Keep in the fridge.

The world's best fruit-based chocolates contain only two ingredients: chocolate and banana!

CHOCOLATES & CONFECTIONS

MINT CHOCOLATE SQUARES

MAKES 10–12 PIECES

CHOCOLATE
½ cup grated raw cacao paste
⅓ cup grated cacao butter
3 tablespoons honey or coconut
   syrup
Pinch of sea salt

MINT FILLING
⅓ cup coconut oil
1–2 teaspoons peppermint extract
   or peppermint oil
½ teaspoon liquid stevia
   or 1 tablespoon honey or
   coconut syrup

If I needed to convince someone how good raw chocolate can be, I would offer them these. All chocolate lovers adore the clean snap of these minty squares.

CHOCOLATE. Melt the cacao paste and cacao butter in the top of a double boiler. Temper the chocolate according to the instructions on page 12 to give it a good "snap" when a piece is broken. Add the honey and salt. Taste and adjust the sweetness.

Pour a thin layer (less than ¼ inch thick) of the chocolate into a dish or into molds, using about half the chocolate. Place in the freezer for 15 minutes to set the chocolate. Make the mint filling while the chocolate is freezing.

FILLING. In another bowl on top of the double boiler, melt the coconut oil and add the peppermint extract and stevia to your liking. Taste and adjust the flavors. Pour the mint filling over the set chocolate, spread quickly, and pop the dish back in the freezer for approximately 5 minutes.

Pour the remaining chocolate over the mint filling and freeze again. Take the mint chocolate from the freezer and let it thaw for a bit before indulging. Keep in the fridge.

PEANUT TOFFEE CHOCOLATES

BASE
⅓ cup grated raw cacao paste
⅓ cup peanut butter
2 tablespoons honey
Coconut oil for greasing

NOUGAT FILLING
⅓ cup peanuts
½ cup almond flour
⅓ cup coconut milk
⅓ cup coconut oil, melted
2 fresh dates, pitted
½ teaspoon vanilla extract

TOFFEE FILLING
⅓ cup peanut butter
⅓ cup honey
¼ cup coconut milk
½ teaspoon vanilla extract
4 fresh dates, pitted
1 dropperful toffee stevia (optional)

PEANUT FILLING
⅓ cup salted peanuts
¼ teaspoon sea salt

CHOCOLATE ICING
¼ cup grated raw cacao paste
2 tablespoons nut butter
¼ cup coconut oil
1 tablespoon honey
¼ teaspoon sea salt

CONTAINER SIZE
About 6 x 8 inches

BASE. Melt the cacao paste in the top of a double boiler. Add the peanut butter and honey. Mix to a smooth paste. Grease a dish or pan with coconut oil and pour the mixture into it. Place in the freezer and prepare the nougat filling.

NOUGAT FILLING. Grind the peanuts in a high-speed blender or food processor. Add the almond flour, coconut milk, coconut oil, dates, and vanilla extract and process. Take the base out of the freezer and pour the filling on top. Return the dish to the freezer and start preparing the toffee and peanut fillings.

TOFFEE & PEANUT FILLINGS. For the toffee filling, process the peanut butter, honey, coconut milk, vanilla extract, dates, and stevia (if using) in a high-speed blender or food processor. For the peanut filling, lightly crush the peanuts with a mortar and pestle and sprinkle with the sea salt. Reserve some crushed peanuts to use as a topping. Take the dish with the nougat-covered base out of the freezer and sprinkle the toffee and peanut fillings over. Smooth with a spoon. Return the dish to the freezer while you prepare the chocolate icing.

CHOCOLATE ICING. Melt the cacao paste in the top of a double boiler. Add the nut butter, coconut oil, and honey. Mix well. Add the sea salt. Bring the dish out of the freezer and pour the chocolate icing evenly over the toffee filling. Pop the beauty back in the freezer for 30 minutes.

Take the dish out of the freezer and flip it onto a serving dish. Pour a bit of warm water over the dish to help the chocolate release from the dish. Flip again and cut into pieces. Sprinkle the reserved crushed peanuts over the chocolate. Serve cold and keep in the fridge.

These delicacies require some care in preparation, but trust me—they're worth it.

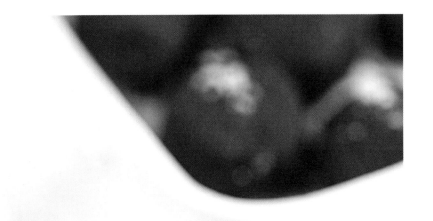

NUT CARAMEL CHOCOLATES

MAKES 15–20 PIECES

CARAMELS
Caramel Spread (page 131)
15–20 pecans
4–5 tablespoons
   unsweetened almond
   or nut butter

ICING
4 ounces unsweetened
   dark or raw chocolate, or
   ½ cup Basic Chocolate,
   (page 12)

ON TOP
Flaky sea salt

CARAMELS. Line a baking sheet with parchment paper or a silicone baking mat.

Prepare the caramel spread using only 1 tablespoon water, to keep the mixture as thick as possible. Drop teaspoon-size dollops of the caramel onto the prepared baking sheet. With moist fingers, mold the caramel into balls. (If the caramel is too runny, pop it in the freezer for a bit.) Press a pecan into each ball and place the sheet in the freezer for 15 minutes.

While the caramel balls are in the freezer, melt the nut butter in the top of a double boiler. Bring the balls out of the freezer and cover each one with melted nut butter. Return to the freezer for about 30 minutes.

ICING. Melt the chocolate in the top of a double boiler, or use the Basic Chocolate.

When time is up, dip the frozen balls into the chocolate icing. Sprinkle with flaky sea salt and return them to the freezer just to set. Bring out, serve, and indulge. Keep in an airtight container in the fridge or freezer.

I love chocolates that combine many elements: a soft filling, a texture that snaps nicely, and something crunchy. Also, a hint of saltiness intrigues me. These chocolates are all of the above and can be created with very simple ingredients.

CARAMEL DROPS

These sweet, dainty drops are fun to enjoy on their own. They can also be mixed into other desserts, like ice cream or a muffin batter.

MAKES ABOUT 80 PIECES

1 cup cashew nuts, soaked overnight
⅓ cup honey
3 fresh dates
½ teaspoon vanilla extract
½ dropperful toffee stevia, or as needed
Pinch of sea salt

Preheat the oven to 180°F. Line a baking sheet with parchment paper or a silicone baking mat.

Drain and rinse the soaked nuts and pour into a high-speed blender or food processor. Add the honey. Peel and pit the dates. (Peeling fresh dates is easy under running water. If the dates seem dry, soak them for a while; dry dates will ruin the mixture.) Add the vanilla extract, stevia, and sea salt. Mix to a smooth paste. Taste and adjust the flavorings as you wish.

Spoon the mixture into a piping bag. Squeeze the bag to force small, flat drops onto the prepared baking sheet. Bake for about 3 hours.

The drops will feel a bit soft and slightly moist, but still solid. Let cool. Enjoy right away, or keep in an airtight container in the fridge.

This is my mother's favorite chocolate, especially when made from bilberries, wild blueberries picked in the forest near my parents' house. However, it makes a fresh and lovely chocolate treat with any kind of blueberries!

BLUEBERRY CHOCOLATE

MAKES 1 LARGE BAR

½ cup grated cacao butter
⅓ cup coconut oil
⅓ cup raw cacao powder
10 drops stevia or
    3 tablespoons honey
Small pinch of sea salt
¼ cup rice bran solubles, or
    tocotrienols (optional)
1 cup fresh blueberries

CONTAINER SIZE
About 5 x 7 inches

Melt the cacao butter and coconut oil in the top of a double boiler. Add the cacao powder, sweetener, and salt. Add the rice bran, if desired, to create a creamy consistency.

Pat the blueberries dry. Pour them into a high-sided container. Pour the prepared chocolate mix over them and place in the fridge for about 1 hour or in the freezer for about 15 minutes. This will let the chocolate firm up without the blueberries freezing. Serve and enjoy! If you leave the chocolate in the freezer for a longer time, thaw it in the fridge before serving to defrost the berries but keep the chocolate firm.

ORANGE MARZIPAN BARS

MAKES 6-8 PIECES

ORANGE MARZIPAN
1 cup almonds
⅓ cup honey or coconut syrup
1 tablespoon grated orange zest
¼ cup fresh orange juice
2 tablespoons almond extract
¼ cup almond flour

CHOCOLATE ICING
4 ounces unsweetened dark
   or raw chocolate, or ½ cup
   Basic Chocolate (page 12)

ON TOP
Blanched almonds
Grated orange zest

MARZIPAN. Grind the almonds to a crumble in a high-speed blender. Add the honey, orange zest, orange juice, and almond extract. Mix well. Pour the mixture into a bowl and stir in the almond flour. This will create a smooth but moldable dough, similar in texture to play dough. Add more flour if needed. Roll into bars and set in the freezer for 15–30 minutes.

ICING. Melt the chocolate in the top of a double boiler, or use the Basic Chocolate.

Use a spoon to drizzle the chocolate icing over the marzipan bars one at a time. Decorate with almonds and/or orange zest. Pop in the fridge or freezer for a bit to set. Serve and enjoy. Keep in the fridge.

Marzipan with chocolate has an exciting elegance to me. I created my own parlor-worthy bars, freshened with a hint of orange.

CHOCOLATES & CONFECTIONS

COCONUT-FILLED CHOCOLATES

A surprise ingredient in these amazingly rich coconut chocolates is potato! You'd never guess when tasting them, but that's the secret to the smooth consistency of the filling.

MAKES ABOUT 8 PIECES

1 potato
3 tablespoons honey or
    coconut syrup
1 teaspoon vanilla extract
1 cup coconut flakes, or as needed
2 tablespoons coconut oil, melted

CHOCOLATE ICING

4 ounces unsweetened dark or
    raw chocolate, or ½ cup Basic
    Chocolate (page 12)

Peel and cut the potato into chunks. Place in a saucepan with water to cover, bring to a boil over medium-high heat, and boil until tender. Drain and mash smooth with a fork. Measure out 3 tablespoons of the mash into a bowl. Add the honey and vanilla extract. Mix well. (The mash will now lose its solid consistency and turn to liquid!) Stir in the coconut flakes and coconut oil. The dough should now be thick enough to form into a ball. Add more coconut flakes if necessary. Divide into 8 pieces and form into small bars on a baking sheet. Pop the sheet in the freezer for 30 minutes to set.

ICING. Prepare the icing by melting the chocolate in a double boiler, or use the Basic Chocolate.

Take the bars out of the freezer and dip them into the chocolate icing or drizzle the icing onto them. Keep in the fridge until serving.

Have ready silicone molds or line a baking sheet with parchment paper or a silicone baking mat.

Crush the nuts with a hand blender or mortar and pestle. Pour the honey into a frying pan and place over medium heat. Stir continuously until the honey starts to foam. Now take note of the time and continue for another 5 minutes. Turn down the heat and add the nut butter. Keep stirring until the liquid starts to thicken. Remove the pan from the heat and quickly add the crushed nuts and the coconut flakes. Mix into a smooth paste.

Divide the mixture among the molds or dollop it onto the prepared baking sheet. If necessary, smooth with a moist knife or a spatula. Dust with sea salt. Place in the fridge for a while to set.

If you made the toffee on a baking sheet, cut it into pieces. Keep the toffees wrapped in parchment paper. They will keep in the fridge for about 2 weeks.

MAKES ABOUT 15 PIECES

⅓ cup almonds and/or
    other nuts
½ cup honey
1 cup unsweetened
    almond butter or other
    nut butter
2 tablespoons coconut
    flakes
Flaky sea salt

SEA SALT TOFFEE CANDIES

A word of warning: I know several toffee lovers who say they so adore these creations of mine that they find themselves preparing a new batch as soon as the previous one runs out.

Delicious rum raisin chocolate is a perfect treat for adults.

RUM RAISIN CHOCOLATE

MAKES ABOUT 3½ OUNCES

¼ cup organic raisins
¼ cup dark rum or bourbon
¼ cup grated raw cacao paste,
   or ¼ cup grated cacao butter
   + ⅓ cup raw cacao powder
⅓ cup coconut oil
2 tablespoons honey
2 tablespoons almond butter
   or other nut butter
½ teaspoon vanilla extract
Pinch of sea salt

Combine the raisins and rum in a pan and bring to a boil. Remove from the heat, cover, and let steep for about 20 minutes. Drain the raisins.

Melt the cacao paste, coconut oil, and honey in the top of a double boiler. Add the almond butter. Melt all and stir into a smooth mixture. Add the drained raisins, vanilla extract, and salt. Divide the mixture among silicone chocolate molds or spread into a layer about ½ inch thick on a plate. Place in the freezer for approximately 30 minutes. Enjoy. Keep in the fridge.

RASPBERRY YOGURT BAR

CHOCOLATE LAYER. Grease a container with coconut oil. Pour the chocolate into it and place in the freezer to set.

COCONUT-RASPBERRY LAYER. Combine the yogurt and coconut in a bowl and mix well. Melt the cacao butter in the top of a double boiler to a runny consistency and stir into the yogurt mixture. Stir in the sweetener. Taste and adjust the flavorings. Bring out the cooled chocolate layer from the freezer and pour the yogurt mixture over the chocolate. Sprinkle with the raspberries and return to the freezer until the chocolate has set, about 30 minutes. Release the chocolate from the pan, break into pieces, serve, and enjoy! Keep in the fridge.

MAKES 1 LARGE BAR

CHOCOLATE LAYER
Coconut oil for greasing
About ½ cup Basic Chocolate
    (page 12)

COCONUT-RASPBERRY LAYER
½ cup coconut yogurt (page 138)
    or other dairy-free yogurt
½ cup coconut flakes
½ cup grated cacao butter
½ teaspoon vanilla stevia,
    or 1 teaspoon vanilla extract
    + 3 tablespoons honey
Handful of fresh aspberries

CONTAINER SIZE
About 8 x 4 inches

You can modify these yogurt chocolate bars with other fresh berries or fruit if you wish.

CHRISTMAS CHOCOLATES

If you want to avoid that stale feeling you get from traditional boxed Christmas chocolates, try these spiced chocolates. A merry Christmas guaranteed!

RAW CHOCOLATE LOG

MAKES 1 LOG

½ cup soft dried figs
2 tablespoons Cognac
5 fresh dates
Handful of pistachio nuts
Handful of almonds
Handful of peanuts

CHOCOLATE MIXTURE

⅓ cup grated raw cacao paste
3 tablespoons coconut oil
3–4 tablespoons raw cacao powder
¼ cup honey or coconut syrup
1 teaspoon ground cinnamon
1 teaspoon ground cloves
Pinch of sea salt

Dice the figs and cut out the stems. Combine with the Cognac in a high-speed blender or food processor and purée. Pit the dates and cut them into small pieces. Crush the nuts with a hand blender or mortar and pestle. Mix the puréed figs, chopped dates, and crushed nuts in a bowl. Set aside.

CHOCOLATE MIXTURE. Melt the cacao paste and coconut oil in the top of a double boiler. Add the cacao powder, honey, cinnamon, cloves, and salt. Pour the mixture into the bowl with the fruit and nuts. Stir to combine, then form into a log. Wrap the log with waxed paper, tying the ends tightly. Place in the fridge overnight to set. Cut the chocolate log into ½-inch slices, serve, and enjoy. Keep in the fridge.

SPICY CHOCOLATE BUTTONS

MAKES ABOUT 15 PIECES

½ cup grated raw cacao paste
½ cup grated cacao butter
2 tablespoons eucalyptus honey, or honey +
    a few drops of edible eucalyptus oil
¼ cup raw cacao powder
Pinch of sea salt

ON TOP
Ground cardamom
Cacao nibs
Crushed star anise

Have ready round silicone chocolate molds or a baking sheet lined with parchment paper.

Melt the cacao paste and cacao butter in the top of a double boiler. Add the eucalyptus honey, cacao powder, and salt. Taste and adjust the flavorings. Temper this chocolate according to the instructions on page 12, in order to create a "snapping" consistency.

Pour the tempered chocolate into the molds or onto the prepared baking sheet, creating round slabs about ½ inch thick. Place in the freezer to set the surface a bit, about 10 minutes. Sprinkle with the cardamom, cacao nibs, and crushed star anise. Freeze for 30 minutes. Serve and enjoy. Keep in the fridge.

GINGERBREAD CHOCOLATES

MAKES 10–15 PIECES

1 cup almonds
5 fresh dates
1 teaspoon gingerbread or pumpkin pie
    spice mix
⅓ cup grated cacao butter
3 tablespoons coconut oil
3 tablespoons raw cacao powder
3 tablespoons honey or coconut syrup
Pinch of sea salt

Grind the almonds in a high-speed blender or food processor, then transfer to a bowl. Pit the dates and cut them into a bowl with kitchen scissors. Add the gingerbread spice mix. Melt the cacao butter and coconut oil in the top of a double boiler and pour into a larger bowl if necessary. Add the cacao powder, honey, and salt. Pour into the blender with the almonds and dates. Mix well to form a dough. Taste and adjust the flavorings. Place in the freezer for 15 minutes to firm up.

Make balls of the firmed dough and roll out to ½-inch thickness between 2 sheets of parchment paper. Cut out desired shapes with cookie cutters. If the dough gets too soft, place it in the freezer to cool it down. Place the gingerbread cookies in the freezer for about 1 hour. Bring out a bit ahead of serving to let them warm up. Keep in the fridge.

FIG FUDGE

MAKES 12–16 PIECES

¼ cup cashew butter or
    other nut butter
3 tablespoons coconut oil
    + oil for greasing
5 dried figs, stemmed
¼ cup raw cacao powder
¼ cup honey or coconut syrup
1 teaspoon vanilla extract
¼ teaspoon sea salt
1–2 tablespoons water, if needed

CONTAINER SIZE
About 4 x 6 inches

This fudge is so easy to make and the consistency is like creamy caramel! Try it with other dried fruit, too.

Melt the nut butter and 3 tablespoons coconut oil in the top of a double boiler. Reserve a teaspoonful for decorating later. Pour into a high-speed blender or food processor, cut in the figs with kitchen scissors, and add the cacao powder, honey, vanilla extract, and salt. Purée until smooth. Add a tablespoon or two of water if the mixture seems too thick.

Grease a container with coconut oil and spoon in the mixture. Drip the reserved nut butter mixture on top. Place in the freezer for a few hours. Once the fudge is set, bring it back to room temperature and cut it into squares, serve, and enjoy. Keep in the fridge or the freezer.

Chocolate puffed rice treats were my ultimate favorite when I was a child. And even nowadays I can easily down this whole batch in one sitting, if no one is watching!

CHOCOLATE PUFFED RICE SQUARES

Melt the cacao butter and coconut oil in the top of a double boiler. Add the honey and almond or nut butter. Mix in the raw cacao powder and rice bran (if using) for creamier consistency. Add the vanilla stevia and salt.

Spread the puffed rice in a high-sided dish or pan, pour the chocolate mixture on top, and stir to mix. Place in the freezer to set for about 30 minutes. Bring to room temperature, cut into pieces, and enjoy.

MAKES 8 SQUARES

⅓ cup grated cacao butter
3 tablespoons coconut oil
¼ cup local organic honey or
    coconut syrup
2 tablespoons nut or
    peanut butter or Vanilla
    Coconut Butter (page 126)
⅓ cup raw cacao powder
3 tablespoons rice bran solubles,
    or tocotrienols (optional)
5 drops of vanilla stevia, or
    ½ teaspoon pure vanilla powder
Pinch of sea salt
1½ cups puffed rice

CONTAINER SIZE
About 5 x 8 inches

LICORICE TRUFFLES

I am a huge fan of the licorice-chocolate combo. I created this recipe after falling in love with soft licorice covered in chocolate.

MAKES 8–10 PIECES

LICORICE BALLS
½ cup almonds
2 tablespoons chia seeds
5 tablespoons black sesame seeds
4 dried figs, stemmed
2 prunes, pitted
1 tablespoon licorice powder
½ teaspoon vanilla extract
1 teaspoon honey or coconut syrup
Pinch of sea salt

CHOCOLATE ICING
½ cup grated raw cacao paste
1 teaspoon coconut oil
1 tablespoon honey
Pinch of sea salt

ON TOP
Licorice powder

BALLS. Grind the almonds in a high-speed blender or food processor to a fine crumble. Add the chia seeds, sesame seeds, figs, prunes, licorice powder, vanilla extract, honey, and salt and blend to a smooth dough. Taste and adjust the licorice or honey to your liking. Form small balls of the dough. Place them in the freezer for a bit to set, and make the chocolate icing in the meantime.

ICING. Melt the cacao paste and coconut oil in the top of a double boiler to a runny consistency. Add the sweetener and salt.

Bring the licorice balls out of the freezer and use a fork to dip them in the chocolate icing, letting the excess drip back into the bowl. Sprinkle the truffles with licorice powder. Return the truffles to the freezer for about 15 minutes to firm up the icing. Keep in the fridge.

CHOCOLATES & CONFECTIONS

MINT CHOCOLATE TRUFFLES

MAKES ABOUT 8 PIECES

MACADAMIA BALLS
1 cup macadamia nuts
3 tablespoons honey
or coconut syrup
8 fresh mint leaves
½ tablespoon raw cacao nibs or
chopped raw cacao paste

CHOCOLATE ICING
2 tablespoons grated cacao butter
2 tablespoons coconut oil
⅓ raw cacao powder
3 tablespoons honey
or coconut syrup
1 teaspoon peppermint oil
Pinch of sea salt

These truffles are truly magic! Macadamia nuts create a rich filling, the perfect counterpoint to the fresh mint flavor and "snap" of the chocolate coating. They will make you return to the fridge again and again.

MACADAMIA BALLS. Chop the nuts in a high-speed blender or food processor. Add the sweetener. Use kitchen scissors to shred the mint leaves into the workbowl and blend to a smooth mixture. Scrape into a bowl and mix in the cacao nibs. Form small balls of the dough and place in the freezer to set for about 15 minutes.

CHOCOLATE ICING. Melt the cacao butter and coconut oil in the top of a double boiler. Stir in the cacao powder, honey, peppermint oil, and salt.

Bring the macadamia balls out of the freezer and use a fork to dip them in the chocolate icing, letting the excess icing drip back into the bowl. If you want the chocolate coating to be thicker, you can dip the balls in the chocolate repeatedly after each layer of icing has set. Freeze the balls for about 30 minutes. Serve and enjoy.

MILK CHOCOLATE DELICACIES

If you find regular dark raw chocolate too strong for your liking, try these milk chocolate recipes. Children like these better, too. These chocolates can't handle warmth as well as others, so keep them in the fridge or the freezer when not serving.

COCONUT MILK CHOCOLATE

MAKES ABOUT 7 OUNCES

1 whole coconut
½ cup grated cacao butter
¼ cup coconut oil
3–4 tablespoons honey or coconut
    syrup
⅓ cup raw cacao powder
½ teaspoon pure vanilla powder
Pinch of sea salt
A few drops of vanilla stevia
3 tablespoons coconut cream or
    coconut water

Preheat the oven to 300°F and have ready some silicone chocolate molds. Drill a hole into an "eye" of the coconut. Pour the coconut water into a bowl. Bake the empty coconut shell for about 20 minutes. Use a hammer to tap the coconut on its equator, which will crack the shell. Cut the coconut meat from the shell and grate about ¼ cup of the coconut meat into a blender or food processor.

Melt the cacao butter and coconut oil in the top of a double boiler. Add the honey, cacao powder, vanilla powder, sea salt, and stevia to taste. Mix well. Taste and adjust the flavorings. Add this chocolate mixture to the grated coconut, along with the coconut cream, and blend to a smooth consistency.

Pour the mixture into chocolate molds and set in the freezer until the chocolate has firmed, 30 minutes or more. Bring to room temperature and enjoy. Keep in the fridge or freezer.

KIDS' CHOICE CHOCOLATE

MAKES ABOUT 7 OUNCES

½ cup cashew nuts or a mix of
    cashew + macadamia nuts
½ cup grated cacao butter
⅓ cup coconut oil
⅓ cup raw cacao powder
⅓ cup honey or coconut syrup
1 teaspoon vanilla extract or
    powder
Pinch of sea salt

Soak the cashew nuts for a few hours if your blender is not very powerful. Otherwise you can use them as they are.

Have ready some silicone chocolate molds or line a baking pan with plastic wrap or aluminum foil. Melt the cacao butter and coconut oil in the top of a double boiler. Add the cacao powder, honey, vanilla extract, and salt. Combine the chocolate mixture and nuts in the blender or food processor and mix to a smooth paste. Taste and adjust the flavorings.

Pour the chocolate into the molds or prepared pan. Freeze until the chocolate has firmed up, about 1 hour. Bring to room temperature, cut to pieces, serve, and enjoy. Keep in the fridge or the freezer.

FRUIT LEATHER

When you're in the mood for a sweet, these apple and vanilla strawberry fruit leathers are perfect to snack on.

CARAMEL APPLE LEATHER

MAKES ABOUT 6 STRIPS

Cacao butter for greasing, if needed
4 organic apples, stemmed + cored
5 fresh dates, pitted + chopped
1 dropperful toffee stevia
½ cup water

VANILLA STRAWBERRY LEATHER

MAKES ABOUT 6 STRIPS

Cacao butter for greasing, if needed
2 cups fresh strawberries
1 dropperful vanilla stevia,
    or 1 tablespoon honey +
    ½ teaspoon pure vanilla powder

Preheat the oven to 180°F and line a baking sheet with a silicone baking mat or parchment paper greased with cacao butter.

Chop the apples or strawberries. (Sour apples should be boiled for about 5 minutes to make sure that the strips don't get holes in them.) Put the apples or strawberries into a blender and add the rest of the ingredients, depending on which flavor you are making. Mix to a smooth paste. Taste and adjust the flavorings.

Spread the fruit paste evenly on the prepared baking sheet. Make sure not to spread it too thin, so the fruit leather doesn't dry out too much. Put in the oven to dry for 3–4 hours. The fruit leather is ready when the surface is no longer moist. Let the leather cool, take it from the sheet, and cut into strips. Keep in an airtight container.

RASPBERRY STICKS

MAKES ABOUT 10 STICKS

1 cup freeze-dried raspberries
2 cups fresh dates

Preheat the oven to 180°F. Line a baking sheet with parchment paper or a silicone baking mat.

Grind the freeze-dried raspberries in a blender to a fine powder. Pit and peel the dates. (Peeling fresh dates is easy under running water.) Add the dates to the blender and purée.

Spoon the mixture into a piping bag. Squeeze onto the prepared baking sheet into ½-inch strips. Bake until a bit firm, 3–4 hours. Cooled, ready-to-eat raspberry sticks have a similar consistency to licorice sticks. Remove the sticks from the oven, let cool, and enjoy. Keep in an airtight container in the fridge.

I created these chewy candy sticks for my four-year-old daughter, who loves all things pink and berry. This recipe can also be made with freeze-dried strawberries or pineapple.

FAT LICORICE CANDIES

MAKES ABOUT 1 CUP

1 cup pitted soft dried prunes
½ cup soaked cashew nuts
½ cup soft dried figs
½ cup water, or as needed
4–5 tablespoons licorice
    powder
1 tablespoon vanilla extract
1 dropperful vanilla stevia
¼ teaspoon sea salt

I'd been dreaming of homemade soft licorice candies, and one evening this just came to me. With a few adjustments, it developed into a brilliant treat. Add a pinch of salt if you like salty licorice. If you are allergic to nuts, you can replace the nuts with figs and prunes.

Soak the prunes, nuts, and figs in water to cover for about 1 hour.

Preheat the oven to 180°F and position a rack in the center of the oven. Drain and rinse the soaked prunes, nuts, and figs and place in a high-speed blender or food processor. Purée, adding ½ cup water or as needed to get the consistency smooth. The mixture should remain as thick as possible. Add the licorice powder, vanilla extract, stevia, and salt and blend. Taste and adjust the flavorings.

Line a baking sheet with parchment paper and spoon the mixture into a piping bag. Squeeze onto the sheet into long strips about ½ inch thick. Bake for 3–4 hours, depending on the thickness of the licorice. You can check if they are done by cutting a small piece of a licorice stick and letting it cool. Finished licorices will be firm but not hard, and slightly sticky. Longer baking time gives you chewier licorice. When they are ready, remove from the oven, let cool, and cut into pieces. Keep in an airtight container in the fridge.

VANILLA COCONUT BUTTONS WITH HEARTS OF CHOCOLATE

MAKES 15–20 PIECES

COCONUT BUTTER MIXTURE

1 cup Vanilla Coconut Butter
(page 126) or store-bought
coconut butter

2 tablespoons coconut oil

2 tablespoons honey, or
½ dropperful vanilla stevia

2 tablespoons fresh lemon juice

1 teaspoon pure vanilla powder
(if using store-bought coconut
butter)

**CHOCOLATE ALMOND BUTTER
FILLING**

½ cup Chocolate Almond Butter
(page 127) or store-bought nut
or peanut butter

2 tablespoons raw cacao powder
(if using store-bought nut
butter)

1 tablespoon honey (if using store-
bought nut butter)

Pinch of sea salt (if using store-
bought nut butter)

Have ready round silicone chocolate molds.

COCONUT BUTTER MIXTURE. Melt the coconut butter, coconut oil, and honey in the top of a double boiler. Add the lemon juice and, if using store-bought coconut butter, vanilla. Stir into a smooth paste. Taste and adjust the flavorings.

FILLING. Use another bowl on top of the double boiler to warm the nut butter to a soft consistency. If using store-bought nut butter, mix in the cacao powder, honey, and salt.

Pour some of the white coconut butter mixture into a mold. Add a dollop of nut butter filling and cover with more coconut butter mix. When all the candies are assembled, place the molds in the freezer for close to an hour. Bring to room temperature, serve, and enjoy! Keep in the fridge in an airtight container.

I love these beautiful little white stars for their looks but also for their taste. The rich chocolate almond butter heart is a great complement to the coconut butter shell.

CAKES
&
PIES

STRAWBERRY ROSE CAKE

CAKE BASE

1½ cups almonds
6 fresh dates + 1 more if needed
2 tablespoons raw cacao powder
Pinch of rose salt
Honey, if needed

STRAWBERRY FILLING

1 cup cashew nuts
1 cup fresh or frozen strawberries
1 ripe banana, peeled and chopped
1 tablespoon rose extract or
    rosewater
1 teaspoon pure vanilla powder,
    or seeds from 1 vanilla bean
Juice of 1 lemon
2–4 tablespoons honey or coconut
    syrup
⅓ cup grated cacao butter
⅓ cup coconut oil

CHOCOLATE ICING

⅔ cup grated cacao butter
3 tablespoons coconut oil
⅓ cup raw cacao powder
2 tablespoons honey or coconut
    syrup
Pinch of sea salt

SPRINGFORM PAN SIZE

8 inches

Originally I created this
cake for Mother's Day.
It has since become one
of the most popular and
most-often-requested
cakes I bake.

CAKE BASE. Line the bottom of a springform pan with parchment paper. Grind the almonds and 6 dates in a high-speed blender or food processor until smooth. Add the cacao powder and salt and blend. If the dough feels too dry, mix in another date or add a bit of honey. The dough may feel a little sticky and should be moldable, not runny. Press half of the dough into the pan firmly.

STRAWBERRY FILLING. If your blender is not very powerful, soak the nuts for about 1 hour. This will make them easier to purée. If you use frozen strawberries, thaw them and drain any excess liquid. Combine the strawberries, banana, and cashew nuts in the blender or food processor and blend umtil smooth. Add the rose extract, vanilla, lemon juice, and honey. Mix well. Melt the cacao butter and coconut oil in the top of a double boiler. Pour into the workbowl with the other ingredients and mix well. Pour the filling over the cake base in the pan. Even it out by tipping the pan from side to side. Place the pan in the freezer for a few hours to firm up.

Bring the cake out when it has set. Remove the cake from the pan and place on a serving plate. Let the cake soften for a while you prepare the chocolate icing.

CHOCOLATE ICING. Melt the cacao butter and coconut oil in the top of a double boiler. Stir in the raw cacao powder, honey, and salt until smooth. Taste and adjust the sweetness, if desired. Spread the icing over the cake, letting it drip over the sides. Serve cool, and keep in the fridge.

In its simplicity, this cake is best when served partially frozen. If you are allergic to nuts, replace the almond flour with coconut flour.

FROSTBITTEN BANANA CAKE

CAKE BASE
½ cup almond flour or ground
  almonds
½ cup coconut flakes or
  shredded coconut
3–4 tablespoons honey or
  coconut syrup
Pinch of sea salt

ICING
3–4 ripe bananas, peeled
  and chopped
Juice of ½ lemon
⅓ cup almond flour or ground
  almonds
1 dropperful vanilla stevia,
  or 2 tablespoons honey +
  1 teaspoon vanilla extract
Pinch of sea salt
⅓ cup coconut oil, melted

ON TOP
Coconut flakes or ground
  coconut

SPRINGFORM PAN SIZE
8 inches

CAKE BASE. Line the bottom of a springform cake pan with parchment paper. Use a high-speed blender or food processor to mix the almond flour with the coconut flakes, honey, and salt to a smooth mixture. The texture should be easily moldable, neither too flaky and dry nor too loose and wet. Pour the mixture into the prepared pan and press it firmly into the pan.

ICING. Use the blender to process the bananas, lemon juice, almond flour, stevia, salt, and coconut oil to a smooth and fluffy mixture. Taste and adjust the flavorings. Pour the icing over the cake base. Smooth with a spoon or by tapping the pan a few times on a table or countertop.

Place the pan in the freezer for a few hours. Once the cake has set, remove the cake from the pan and place it on a serving plate. Sprinkle with coconut flakes. Serve slightly softened, and keep any leftover cake in the freezer.

LOTTA'S CAKE

CAKE

Coconut oil for greasing pan

⅔ cup coconut flour

¼ cup almond flour

½ cup raw cacao powder

2 teaspoons baking powder

1 teaspoon vanilla powder

6 eggs

⅓ cup honey

⅓ cup coconut sugar

1 cup oat milk

FILLING

1 cup Peanut Butter Spread
(page 134)

2 tablespoons almond liquor or
almond extract

Double batch Whipped Coconut
Cream (page 132)

3 ripe bananas

ON TOP

Edible flowers

Coconut flour

SPRINGFORM PAN SIZE

8 inches

Preheat the oven to 350°F and position a rack in the center of the oven. Line the bottom of a springform cake pan with parchment paper and grease the sides with coconut oil.

Mix the coconut flour, almond flour, cacao powder, baking powder, and vanilla powder in a bowl. Separate the egg whites and yolks into separate bowls. Whip the egg whites until foamy. Add the honey and coconut sugar to the yolks in the other bowl. Mix for a few minutes until the mixture is fluffy and light in color. Mix the dry ingredients in with the yolk mixture and add in the oat milk. Carefully fold in the egg whites, keeping the mixture fluffy.

Pour the mixture into the prepared cake pan and bake for about 35 minutes. Prepare the fillings while the cake bakes.

Make the peanut butter spread and add 2 tablespoons almond liquor. Make a double batch of whipped coconut cream. Peel and chop the bananas.

Remove the cake from the oven and let cool. Take the cake out of the pan, using a knife to help release it from the sides, if needed. Cut the cake horizontally into 3 layers. Spread the peanut butter spread atop 2 of the layers, sprinkle the chopped bananas over the peanut butter spread, and dollop plenty of the whipped coconut cream on top of the bananas. Stack the cake layers, finishing with the unfrosted one. Decorate with flowers and dust with coconut flour.

I designed this cake for my
dear friend Lotta's wedding,
although on that occasion
I made it three times as big.
The cake was such a success
it made it into the book at
the last moment.

This fresh lime cake will take care of any hankering for a sweet, without being too much. My husband is a big fan, even though he usually does not go in for sweets.

LIME CHOCOLATE CAKE

CAKE BASE

2 cups almonds
6 tablespoons nut butter
⅓ cup honey or coconut
   syrup
⅓ cup raw cacao powder
Pinch of sea salt

ICING

2 large avocados, peeled
   and chopped
2 ripe bananas, peeled and
   chopped
3–5 tablespoons honey or
   coconut syrup
1 tablespoon grated lime zest
⅓ cup fresh lime juice
½ teaspoon pure vanilla
   powder
¼ cup grated cacao butter
2 tablespoons coconut oil

ON TOP

Raw cacao powder or grated
   cacao paste
Grated lime zest

SPRINGFORM PAN SIZE

8 inches

CAKE BASE. Line the bottom of a springform pan with parchment paper.

Grind the almonds in a high-speed blender or food processor to a crumble. Melt the nut butter and honey in the top of a double boiler to a runny consistency. Add the nut butter mixture, cacao powder, and salt to the blender and blend until smooth. If your blender is struggling with the load, transfer the mass into a bowl and use your hands.

Press the mixture into the prepared pan evenly, lining the sides as well as the bottom.

ICING. Clean and dry your blender. Put in the avocados and bananas. Add honey to taste, the lime zest and juice, and the vanilla powder. Blend to a smooth mixture. Melt the cacao butter and coconut oil in the top of a double boiler and pour in with the rest. Blend well. Taste and adjust the flavorings. Pour the icing over the cake base and place in the freezer to set for about 1 hour.

Bring the cake out of the freezer, remove it from the pan, set it on a serving dish, and let it warm a bit before serving. Sprinkle with cacao powder and a bit of lime zest. Serve quickly while still cool. Keep in the fridge.

This cake, with its banana filling veiled in whipped coconut cream, is by far the most popular of my raw cakes. I get requests for the recipe all the time. I've tasted it made by others, and it always works like a dream!

WHIPPED COCONUT CREAM CHOCOLATE CAKE

Whipped Coconut Cream
(page 132)

CAKE BASE
3 cups almonds, or as needed
½ cup coconut flakes, or as
    needed
1 ripe banana, peeled and
    chopped
5 tablespoons raw cacao
    powder
3 tablespoons honey or
    coconut syrup
Pinch of sea salt

CHOCOLATE FILLING
⅓ cup grated cacao butter
1 tablespoon coconut oil
⅓ cup nut butter
3 tablespoons raw cacao
    powder
3 tablespoons organic honey
    or coconut syrup
Pinch of salt

1–2 ripe bananas
Desiccated coconut or
    coconut flakes

SPRINGFORM PAN SIZE
8 inches

Prepare the whipped coconut cream according to the recipe on page 132. Place in the fridge while you prepare the cake.

CAKE BASE. Grind the almonds in a blender. Add the coconut flakes and the banana. Blend well to a smooth mixture. Add the raw cacao powder, sweetener, and salt. Mix well. The dough should be quite dry but easily moldable. If necessary, add more ground almonds and coconut flakes. Taste and adjust the sweetness if you wish.

CHOCOLATE FILLING. Melt the cacao butter and coconut oil in the top of a double boiler. Stir in the nut butter, cacao powder, honey, and salt. Mix well. Taste and adjust the flavorings.

Line the bottom of a springform pan with parchment paper. Press half of the cake base of the pan firmly and evenly into the pan. Spread a thin layer of the chocolate filling on top. Leave the rest of the filling in the double boiler to wait. Place the pan in the freezer until the chocolate has firmed up, about 15 minutes. Bring the pan back out and press the rest of the cake base on top of the chocolate layer. Pour the remainder of the chocolate filling on top and return to the freezer.

When the chocolate is firm, bring the pan out of the freezer and remove the cake from the pan. Place it on the serving plate and leave to warm up for a bit. Slice up the banana(s) and cover the cake with banana slices. Take the whipped coconut cream out of the fridge and stir a little. Spread it over the cake. Sprinkle with coconut and serve.

RAW CARROT CAKE

BASE

2 carrots, peeled and chopped
1½ cups walnuts
½ cup raisins
½ cup coconut flakes
3 tablespoons fresh orange juice
2–4 tablespoons honey or coconut syrup
1 teaspoon vanilla extract
1 teaspoon ground cinnamon
½ teaspoon ground cardamom

ICING

1 cup cashews (soaked for 1 hour, if desired)
2 tablespoons coconut oil, melted
2 tablespoons fresh lemon juice
2 tablespoons honey or coconut syrup
1 teaspoon vanilla extract
1 teaspoon grated orange zest
1 tablespoon water, if needed

ON TOP

Walnuts, orange zest, and ground cinnamon

PAN SIZE

About 7 inches square

CAKE BASE. Grind the carrots into popcorn-sized pieces in a high-speed blender or food processor. Add the raisins, coconut flakes, orange juice, honey, vanilla extract, cinnamon, and cardamom and pulse to mix. The batter should remain coarse and not blend to a sticky clump. Taste and adjust the flavorings.

Line a square baking pan with parchment paper or plastic wrap, letting it drape over the sides. Scoop the batter into the prepared pan and spread evenly.

ICING. Soak the cashews, if you like, to make them easier to digest and blend. Drain and rinse. Add the nuts, coconut oil, lemon juice, sweetener, vanilla extract, and orange zest to the blender or food processor and blend until smooth. If needed, add a little water. The icing should resemble cream cheese, thick and sticky. Spread the icing over the cake.

Pop the cake in the freezer for a few hours. Bring back to room temperature and remove by lifting the parchment paper or plastic wrap sides. Let the cake warm up for a bit. Decorate with walnuts, orange zest, and cinnamon. Cut into pieces, serve, and enjoy!

Accented with warm spices, this carrot cake is one of my favorites. It always works and reminds very much of the traditional version.

CAKES & PIES

CHERRY DREAM CAKE

I love the classic chocolate cherry shakes of the eighties! That's what inspired the flavors for this cake.

CAKE BATTER. Soak the nuts for 1–5 hours. Drain and rinse the nuts. Melt the cacao butter in the top of a double boiler. Scrape the thick white layer of coconut cream from the can of coconut milk into a high-speed blender or food processor. Add the soaked nuts, melted cacao butter, coconut oil, stevia, and honey and blend well, until the mixture is even and smooth. Taste and adjust the sweetness if you wish.

Pour about two-thirds of the batter into a larger bowl and the remaining one-third into a smaller one.

Line the bottom of a springform pan with parchment paper.

FLAVORINGS. To the smaller bowl of batter, add the cacao powder, grated chocolate, almond extract, and honey. Mix well. Pour the chocolate batter into the prepared pan. Place in the freezer until the surface has set, about 15 minutes.

Bring the pan out of the freezer. Add the cherries to the larger bowl of batter and mix quickly. Pour the cherry mixture over the chocolate layer in the pan. Return the cake to the freezer for about 30 minutes. Bring the cake out of the freezer, remove from the pan, and place on a serving plate. Serve slightly softened, and keep any leftover cake in the fridge or freezer.

CAKE BATTER
1½ cups soaked cashew or
  macadamia nuts
½ cup grated cacao butter
1 can full-fat coconut milk,
  refrigerated overnight
2 tablespoons coconut oil
1 teaspoon liquid vanilla
  stevia, or stevia +
  1 tablespoon vanilla
  extract
1 tablespoon honey or
  coconut syrup

FLAVORINGS
¼ cup raw cacao powder
¼ cup grated chocolate
  or raw cacao nibs
1 tablespoon almond extract
⅓ cup honey or coconut syrup
1¼ cups fresh cherries,
  halved and pitted

SPRINGFORM PAN SIZE
8 inches

Prepare the whipped coconut cream; cover and refrigerate.

PANCAKE. Preheat the oven to 400°F and position a rack in the center of the oven. Break the eggs into a high-speed blender or food processor and add the flours, oat milk, honey, banana, psyllium husk powder, baking powder, vanilla extract, and salt. Blend until smooth. Pour the mixture onto a rimmed baking sheet and bake for about 30 minutes. When the pancake is golden with brown spots, remove it from the oven.

Cut the pancake to 9 evenly sized pieces. Pile the pieces on a serving platter or plate, layering honey, banana slices, and berries between the pieces. Sprinkle berries on top and spoon plenty of whipped coconut cream over them. (Best to add the whipped coconut cream on top of the berries and not directly on the warm pancake, or else it will melt away.) Sprinkle more berries on top and serve.

This cake was conceived as a birthday cake for myself. It has since become one of my summertime favorites.

GORGEOUS PANCAKE CAKE

Whipped Coconut Cream
(page 132)

PANCAKE
3 large eggs
1 cup almond flour
¼ cup coconut flour
½ cup buckwheat flour
3 cups oat milk or other milk
    alternative (page 137)
1 tablespoon honey or
    coconut syrup
1 ripe banana, peeled and
    chopped
1 teaspoon psyllium husk
    powder
1 teaspoon baking powder
2 teaspoons vanilla extract
Pinch of sea salt

Honey or coconut syrup
2 ripe bananas, peeled and
    sliced
Fresh berries and fruit,
    such as raspberries,
    strawberries, and cherries

CAKES & PIES

BLUEBERRY DREAM CAKE

CAKE BASE
1 cup almonds
½ cup toasted and peeled
    hazelnuts
5–7 soft fresh dates, pitted
¼ teaspoon ground
    cardamom

FILLING
3 ripe bananas, peeled
    and sliced
1 cup fresh blueberries
1 teaspoon vanilla extract
1 tablespoon honey or
    coconut syrup
½ cup coconut oil, melted

ON TOP
Whipped Coconut Cream
    (page 132)
Fresh blueberries

SPRINGFORM PAN SIZE
8 inches

This cake is for everyone who wants to try their hand at raw cakes. It's a classic that never lets you down.

CAKE BASE. Use a high-speed blender or food processor to grind the almonds and hazelnuts into a fine crumble. Use kitchen scissors to cut in the dates. Add the cardamom and blend until smooth.

Line the bottom of a springform pan with parchment paper. Press the cake base into the pan as a dense layer.

FILLING. Use a mixer to blend the bananas and blueberries to a smooth mash. Add the vanilla, honey, and coconut oil. Mix until smooth. Pour the mixture over the cake base and even it out with a spoon or by tapping the pan a few times on a table or countertop. Place the pan in the freezer to set until the filling is solid, a few hours. Prepare the whipped coconut cream.

Spoon plenty of the whipped coconut cream over the cake, sprinkle blueberries on top, serve, and enjoy! Keep in the fridge.

THE PERFECT
APPLE PIE

PIE BASE
½ cup almonds
½ cup pecans
¾ cup soft raisins
½ teaspoon cardamom

SYRUP
1 orange
1 apple
½ cup fresh dates, pitted
Juice of 1 lemon
1–2 teaspoons ground
    cinnamon
1 teaspoon vanilla extract
Water as needed

FILLING
4 apples, cored and chopped

PAN SIZE
8 inches

I once had a similar cake in a coffeehouse, and it blew my mind. I tried to replicate the taste at home and think I did a pretty good job. In the process, I nearly managed to develop an addiction.

PIE BASE. Grind the almonds and pecans in a high-speed blender or food processor to a crumble. Add the raisins and cardamom. Mix to a quite dry but sticky dough. Press the base dough into a high-sided tart pan with a removable base. Use the dough to line the sides as well.

SYRUP. Peel, seed, and chop the orange into small pieces. Core and chop the apple. Use a high-speed blender or food processor to blend the orange, apple, dates, lemon juice, cinnamon, and vanilla extract into a smooth syrup, adding a splash of water if needed.

FILLING. Spread the apples over the pie base and cover them with the syrup. Place in the freezer for 30–60 minutes. Serve and enjoy!

Preheat the oven to 350°F. Grease a baking pan or muffin pans, or use paper muffin liners.

Mix all the dry ingredients in a bowl: coconut sugar, flours, cacao powder, baking powder, vanilla powder, salt, walnuts, and cacao butter.

Use another bowl to mix the wet ingredients: eggs, water, and butter. Pour this mixture over the dry ingredients and stir well.

Pour the batter into the prepared pan(s) and bake for 20–30 minutes. Use a toothpick to test if the brownie is done: when done, there will be no batter sticking to the toothpick.

If you wish, you can cover the brownie with one of the easy chocolate icings. Cut into squares to serve.

This rich chocolate brownie is studded with crunchy nuts. The mix makes a lovely present for friends. I put the dry ingredients into a glass jar and present it with a card listing the wet ingredients to add.

NUT BROWNIE

Coconut oil for greasing
1 cup coconut sugar
½ cup almond flour
¼ cup buckwheat flour
½ cup raw cacao powder
1 teaspoon baking powder
1 teaspoon vanilla powder
½ teaspoon sea salt
½ cup crushed walnuts
½ cup grated cacao butter
3 large eggs
3 tablespoons water
½ cup butter, melted
Easy Chocolate Icing, page 128
    or 129 (optional)

BAKING PAN SIZE
About 8 x 10 inches (you can
    also use muffin pans)

CAKE. Preheat the oven to 350°F and position a rack in the center of the oven. Grease a round cake pan or muffin pans, or use paper muffin liners. Mix the rice flour, coconut flour, baking powder, and poppy seeds in a bowl. Add the salt. In another bowl, whisk the honey and coconut oil. Whisk in the eggs one at a time. Add the coconut milk then the lemon zest and juice. If you like, add a few drops of stevia to sweeten. The batter should be thick but easy to spoon, much like oatmeal porridge. Add flour or liquid if needed.

Pour the batter into the prepared cake pan or muffin pans. Bake in the center of the oven until golden brown, 20–25 minutes.

Remove the cake from the oven and let cool. Prepare the whipped coconut cream.

Remove the cooled cake from the pan, pour the whipped coconut cream over it, and decorate with some lemon zest.

Sunshine in the form of cake, for your pleasure! Filled with flavor, this fresh crumbly cake is dappled with poppy seeds. You can also make muffins instead of a cake.

LEMON POPPYSEED CAKE

CAKE
½ cup coconut oil, melted + oil for greasing
½ cup rice flour
¼ cup coconut flour
1 teaspoon baking powder
1 tablespoon poppy seeds
Pinch of sea salt
⅓ cup honey (or coconut syrup)
4 large eggs
½ cup coconut milk or other milk alternative (see page 137)
Grated zest of 1 lemon
Juice of ½ lemon
A few drops of stevia (optional)

Whipped Coconut Cream (page 132)

ON TOP
Grated lemon zest

CAKE PAN SIZE
8 inches (you can also use muffin pans)

CAKES & PIES

This one is perfect for sweets lovers. When I had a taste for the first time, I nearly burst into tears of happiness.

CARAMEL MUD PIE

PIE BASE
½ cup coconut oil, melted
   + more for greasing
¾ cup coconut flour
½ cup almond flour
⅓ cup raw cacao powder
1 teaspoon baking powder
Pinch of sea salt

⅓ cup honey or coconut
   syrup or sugar
2 large eggs, beaten
1 teaspoon vanilla extract

CHOCOLATE FILLING
2 sweet potatoes (about
   1 lb each)
½ cup coconut oil, melted
⅓ cup honey or coconut
   syrup
2 large eggs
1 teaspoon vanilla extract
⅓ cup raw cacao powder
2 tablespoons coconut flour
1 teaspoon baking powder
Pinch of sea salt

TOPPING
Caramel Spread (page 131)
Whipped Coconut Cream
   (page 132)

SPRINGFORM PAN SIZE
8 inches

Preheat the oven to 350°F. Line the bottom of a springform pan with parchment paper and grease the sides with coconut oil.

PIE BASE. In one bowl, mix all the dry ingredients: flours, cacao powder, baking powder, and salt. In another bowl, mix all the wet ingredients: coconut oil, honey, eggs, and vanilla extract. Pour the dry ingredients into the wet and mix well. Press the dough evenly into the prepared pan and up the pan sides. Bake the pie base in the oven for 6–8 minutes.

CHOCOLATE FILLING. In the meantime, peel, chop, and steam the sweet potato for the filling. Remove the pie base from the oven and let cool while you prepare the chocolate filling. Leave the oven turned on. Add the steamed sweet potatoes to a high-speed blender or food processor. Add the coconut oil, honey, eggs, and vanilla extract and blend. Add the cacao powder, coconut flour, baking powder, and salt and blend until smooth. Pour the filling over the cooled pie base and return to the oven to bake for about 25 minutes. Let cool and then place the pie in the fridge to set for a few hours.

TOPPING. Prepare the caramel spread and whipped coconut cream. Spread the caramel over the cake and follow with plenty of whipped coconut cream. Serve and enjoy. Keep in the fridge.

PISTACHIO MINT CHOCOLATE BROWNIE

BROWNIE BATTER

⅓ cup coconut oil, melted +
   more for greasing
½ cup flaxseeds + ½ cup water
2 cups canned black beans
½ cup honey or coconut syrup
¾ cup water or milk alternative
   (page 137)
1 teaspoon vanilla extract
⅓ cup coconut flour
⅓ cup almond flour
⅓ cup pistachios
⅓ cup raw cacao powder
2 teaspoons baking powder
Pinch of sea salt

CHOCOLATE ICING

Avocado Chocolate Icing
   (page 129)
1 teaspoon peppermint extract

ON TOP

Crushed pistachios

PAN SIZE

8 x 8 inches

BROWNIE BATTER. Preheat the oven to 400°F and position a rack in the center of the oven. Grease a square baking pan with coconut oil. (If you are making a double amount, you can line a sided baking sheet with parchment paper.)

Soak the flaxseeds in the water until a thick gel forms around them, about 15 minutes. Drain and rinse the canned beans. Combine the flaxseed gel, beans, coconut oil, honey, water, and vanilla extract in a high-speed blender or food processor and blend until smooth. In another bowl, stir together the flours, nuts, cacao powder, baking powder, and salt. Pour this mixture into the workbowl and blend all the ingredients. The batter should be thick but easily spooned.

Pour the batter into the prepared pan. Bake for 30–45 minutes, depending on pan size. The brownie should be dry on the surface but still remain slightly soft inside.

ICING. Prepare the avocado chocolate icing and add the peppermint extract. Let the brownie cool completely before spreading the icing over it. Decorate with crushed pistachios. Cover and refrigerate overnight.

ATTENTION! For this brownie to come out perfect, it's important to let it set in the fridge overnight. This will allow the taste and consistency to develop properly. So make sure to serve and enjoy only the next day! It can be decorated before or after refrigerating.

This minty chocolate brownie undergoes a magical transformation overnight, turning it into a super-tasty and sweet delicacy.

CAKES & PIES

FIG CHOCOLATE TART

TART DOUGH
1 cup almonds
¼ cup gluten-free oats
5 fresh figs
Coconut oil, for greasing

FILLING
8 ounces unsweetened raw or dark
    chocolate, or a double batch
    (1 cup) Basic Chocolate (page 12)
¼ cup almond milk or other milk
    alternative (page 137)

ON TOP
Fresh figs, stemmed and sliced

TART PAN SIZE
10 x 4 inches

Fresh figs and rich chocolate are a match made in heaven!

TART DOUGH. Use a high-speed blender or food processor to grind the almonds and oats to a crumble. Add the chopped figs and blend into a dough. Grease a rectangular tart pan with a removable base with coconut oil and press the dough into the pan. Place the pan in the freezer.

FILLING. In the top of a double boiler, melt the raw or dark chocolate, or use the 1 cup Basic Chocolate. Add the almond milk and mix until smooth. Bring the tart pan out of the freezer and pour the chocolate filling over the dough. Decorate with sliced fresh figs. Return the tart to the freezer to set until the surface has firmed up, about 1 hour. Bring back to room temperature. To help the tart release from the pan, warm the sides with a kitchen towel moistened with warm water. Serve and enjoy! Keep in the fridge.

A lemon pie I enjoyed at a friend's house haunted me, so I created this recipe to reproduce the taste at home. This version is not quite the same—but it may be even better.

LEMON PIE

PIE DOUGH

1 cup Brazil nuts

½ cup almond flour + more
    for dusting

⅓ cup coconut oil, melted + more
    for greasing

4–5 tablespoons honey or
    coconut syrup

Pinch of sea salt

LEMON FILLING

1½ cups cashew nuts,
    soaked for 1 hour

⅓ cup grated cacao butter

¼ cup fresh lemon juice

¼ cup almond milk or oat milk
    (page 137)

1 tablespoon grated lemon zest

2 tablespoons honey or coconut
    syrup

5 fresh dates, pitted

1 teaspoon vanilla extract

½ teaspoon ground turmeric

Whipped Coconut Cream
    (page 132)

SPRINGFORM PAN SIZE

8 inches

PIE DOUGH. Grind the Brazil nuts to a crumbly texture in a high-speed blender or food processor. Add the almond flour, coconut oil, the honey, and salt. Blend into a smooth dough; the consistency should be dry and crumbly, but still easily moldable. If needed, add more almond flour.

Line the bottom of a springform pan with parchment paper. Grease the sides of the pan with coconut oil and dust with almond flour. Press the pie dough into the pan evenly, including up the sides. Place the pan in the freezer for 15 minutes.

FILLING. Rinse the soaked nuts and grind them in the blender. Melt the cacao butter in the top of a double boiler and add to the blender. Add the lemon juice and almond milk and blend until smooth. Add the lemon zest, honey, dates, vanilla extract, and turmeric and mix well. Taste and adjust the flavorings. Bring the cake pan from the freezer and pour the filling over the pie dough. Return to the freezer until the mixture is solid, about 1 hour.

Prepare the whipped coconut cream. Take the pie out of the freezer and decorate by piping some of the whipped coconut cream in rosettes on the pie. Place the pie in the fridge until serving.

MANUKA BLACK CURRANT CAKE

CAKE BASE
1 cup almonds
4–5 fresh dates, pitted
Pinch of sea salt

FILLING
1½ cup almonds, soaked for 1 hour
    and drained
¼ cup almond milk or other milk
    alternative (page 137)
3 tablespoons honey
    (try 2 tablespoons manuka
    honey + 1 tablespoon local
    organic honey)
¼ cup fresh lemon juice
1 teaspoon pure vanilla powder
Water as needed
½ cup coconut oil (replace partly
    with melted cacao butter
    if you don't like the taste of
    coconut), melted

ICING
1 cup fresh black currants
    or blackberries
¼ cup coconut oil, melted
3 tablespoons honey (try
    1 tablespoon manuka honey
    + 2 tablespoons local organic
    honey)
1 teaspoon pure vanilla powder

SPRINGFORM PAN SIZE
8 inches

Manuka honey is the ultimate sweetener, thanks both to its flavor and its health-boosting qualities. In this cake it creamily joins forces with another superfood: local black currants, if you can get them! (Otherwise, try blackberries.) This cake is good for you in so many ways.

CAKE BASE. Line the bottom of a springform pan with parchment paper. Grind the almonds in a high-speed blender or food processor. Add the dates and salt. Blend into a moldable dough. Press the dough firmly into the pan. Next, prepare the filling.

FILLING. Clean the blender and purée the almonds, almond milk, honey, lemon juice, and vanilla powder into smooth paste. Add a bit of water if necessary to keep the blender working. Try to keep the mixture as thick as possible. Pour in the coconut oil. Mix until smooth. Taste and adjust the flavorings. Pour the filling over the cake base and place the pan in the freezer.

ICING. Clean the blender again and purée the black currants, coconut oil, honey, and vanilla powder into a smooth mash. Taste and adjust the flavorings. Bring the cake out of the freezer and pour the icing on top. Return to the freezer for at least 2 hours. Take out and bring to room temperature, serve, and enjoy!

COOKIES, MUFFINS & OTHER SMALL BAKED GOODS

ANISE & FIG COOKIES

MAKES ABOUT 16 COOKIES

1 cup buckwheat flour
½ cup almond flour
½ cup coconut sugar
¼ cup ground flaxseed
1 tablespoon ground star anise
1 teaspoon baking powder
¼ teaspoon sea salt
½ cup oat milk or other milk
   alternative (page 137)
¼ cup coconut oil and/or butter,
   melted
1 teaspoon vanilla extract
½ cup flaked almonds
7 dried figs, chopped into small
   pieces
Water as needed

ON TOP

Licorice powder

Let me present one of my favorite cookies! Anise combined with fig offers a lovely licorice taste. A dusting of licorice powder accents the flavor. The hint of almond makes these cookies heavenly.

Mix the flours, coconut sugar, flaxseed, star anise, baking powder, and sea salt in a bowl. Use another bowl to mix the oat milk, coconut oil, and vanilla extract. Pour the wet mixture in with the dry ingredients. Add the almonds and figs and mix. The dough should be solid, soft, and moldable. Add some water if necessary.

Roll the dough into a log with a diameter of about 2 inches. Wrap in plastic wrap and place in the fridge for 30 minutes or in the freezer for 15 minutes.

Preheat the oven to 350°F and line a baking sheet with parchment paper. Bring the dough log back to room temperature and remove the plastic wrap. Slice the log into ½-inch pieces. Place the pieces on the prepared baking sheet. Sprinkle each with a pinch of licorice powder. Bake for about 10 minutes. Flip the cookies carefully and bake for another 10 minutes. Let cool completely. Serve and enjoy!

LACE COOKIES

MAKES ABOUT 18 COOKIES

¼ cup butter
¼ cup honey or coconut syrup
¼ cup gluten-free oats
¼ cup almond flour
3 tablespoons coconut sugar
½ teaspoon pure vanilla powder
¼ teaspoon sea salt
2 tablespoons grated orange zest
   (optional)

Preheat the oven to 400°F. Line a baking sheet with parchment paper or a silicone baking mat.

Melt the butter and honey in a pan and mix until smooth. Remove the pan from the heat and add the oats, almond flour, coconut sugar, vanilla, salt, and orange zest, if using. Mix well. Dollop onto the prepared baking sheet in teaspoon-sized dabs. Leave plenty of room around each cookie, as they will spread quite a lot. Bake until golden brown, about 8 minutes. They will burn easily, so watch out; undercooked cookies, however, will be too floppy. Let them cool and firm up, then serve and enjoy!

These beautiful paper-thin lace cookies are quick to make. They will appeal to all you Swedish Tosca cookie lovers out there.

These cookies are fun to make and snack on, especially for kids. The banana-nut combo is irresistible.

NUT BANANA COOKIES

Preheat the oven to 350°F and line a baking sheet with parchment paper. Use a blender to grind the nuts to a coarse crumble. Add the bananas. Add the vanilla, cinnamon, cardamom, and salt and keep mixing. Stir in the raisins. Roll tablespoonfuls of the dough into balls and pat into cookies about ¼ inch thick. Place on the prepared baking sheet. Bake for about 20 minutes. To prevent burning, flip the cookies after about 15 minutes. Let cool, serve, and enjoy!

MAKES ABOUT 10 COOKIES

1⅓ cups different kinds of nuts, such as cashews, pecans, and/or walnuts
2 ripe bananas, peeled and chopped
1 teaspoon pure vanilla powder
½ teaspoon ground cinnamon
¼ teaspoon ground cardamom
¼ teaspoon sea salt
Handful of raisins

COOKIES. Preheat the oven to 350°F and position a rack in the center of the oven. Line a baking sheet with parchment paper. Pour the nut flour into a bowl and add the oat flour, cacao powder, baking powder, vanilla powder, tapioca starch (if using), and salt. Melt the butter in the top of a double boiler to a runny consistency and add the honey. Add the egg, if using. Stir this mixture into the dry ingredients. Scoop up the dough in tablespoonfuls, roll into balls, and press to flatten into cookies about ⅜ inch thick. Bake for about 10 minutes. (Be careful not to overbake, or the cookies will dry out.) While the cookies bake, prepare the filling.

FILLING. Melt the nut butter and coconut oil in the top of a double boiler. Add the cacao powder, honey, and vanilla extract and mix well. If the spread feels too runny, pop it in the fridge for a bit.

Take the cookies out of the oven and let cool completely. Build into double-decker cookies by spreading some filling between pairs of cookies. Serve and enjoy. Keep in the fridge.

These chocolate-filled cookies get better with time. Tip! You can double the number of cookies if you double the amount of filling and use it to ice each cookie individually.

CACAO-FILLED HAZELNUT COOKIES

MAKES 6–8 COOKIES

COOKIES

1 cup hazelnut flour or ground hazelnuts

¼ cup oat flour or ground gluten-free oats

½ cup raw cacao powder

1 teaspoon baking powder

1 teaspoon vanilla powder

2 tablespoons tapioca starch, or 1 egg, beaten

½ teaspoon sea salt

½ cup butter and/or coconut oil

5–7 tablespoons honey or coconut syrup

FILLING

¼ cup nut butter

⅓ cup coconut oil

2 tablespoons raw cacao powder

3 tablespoons honey or coconut syrup

½ teaspoon vanilla extract

COOKIES, MUFFINS & OTHER SMALL BAKED GOODS

CRUNCHY CHOCOLATE MUFFINS

MAKES 8–10 MUFFINS

MUFFINS
1½ cups almond flour
½ cup raw cacao powder
¼ cup coconut sugar, or ⅓ cup honey
2 teaspoons baking powder
3 eggs, beaten
½ cup butter and/or coconut oil,
    melted
½ cup oat milk, other milk alternative
    (page 137), or coconut water
    + more if needed
2 teaspoons vanilla extract
Pinch of sea salt
¼ cup raw cacao nibs

Easy Chocolate Icing (page 128 or 129)

ON TOP
Desiccated coconut or coconut flakes

These rich chocolate muffins are deliciously crunchy, thanks to the raw cacao nibs. I get so many compliments on these from other people—and from myself as well.

MUFFINS. Preheat the oven to 350°F and line muffin pans with paper muffin liners. Mix the almond flour, cacao powder, coconut sugar, and baking powder in one bowl. In another bowl, mix the eggs, butter, oat milk, vanilla extract, and salt. Pour the wet ingredients into the dry ingredients and mix well. Stir in the raw cacao nibs. The texture of the dough should be now soft and spoonable, not too liquid. If it feels very dry, add a bit more oat milk. Spoon the dough into muffin pans and bake in the center of the oven for about 25–35 minutes. The muffins can remain slightly soft in the center. Before icing, let the muffins cool completely.

Prepare the icing and Spread on the muffins. Sprinkle with coconut. Serve and enjoy!

NUT BUTTER-COVERED MOCHA MUFFINS

MUFFINS. Preheat the oven to 400°F. Mix the coconut flour, cacao powder, and baking powder together in one bowl. In another bowl, mix the honey, eggs, coconut oil, oat milk, and vanilla extract. Pour into the dry ingredients and mix well. Add the coffee, mix, and let stand for about 5 minutes. The texture of the dough should be soft and spoonable. If it feels very dry, add a bit more oat milk. Spoon into the muffin pans and bake in the center of the oven for about 20 minutes. The muffins can remain slightly soft in the center. Before icing, let the muffins cool completely.

ICING. Melt the butter, peanut butter, and honey in a pot over medium heat until smooth. Stir in the vanilla extract and oat milk. Take the pan off the heat and set a few tablespoons of the mixture aside. Transfer the remaining mixture to a bowl and let cool a bit in the fridge. Use a blender to blend to a fluffy and light icing. Spread over the cooled muffins with a generous touch. Thin the reserved icing with some of the oat milk and spoon it into a piping bag and use it to decorate further. Serve and enjoy!

A friend of mine, Maiju, is a great food lover and, in particular, a sweets lover. I often test my recipes on her. I knew these muffins had passed with flying colors when, after tasting them at a party, she hid a box of them from the other guests.

MAKES ABOUT 10 MUFFINS

MUFFINS
½ cup coconut flour
¼ cup raw cacao powder
2 teaspoons baking powder
⅓ cup honey or coconut syrup
4 large eggs, beaten
½ cup coconut oil, melted
½ cup oat milk or other milk
    alternative (page 137) + more if
    needed
1 teaspoon vanilla extract
⅓ cup strong coffee

ICING
½ cup butter or coconut oil
½ cup unsweetened peanut butter
¼ cup or coconut syrup
1 teaspoon vanilla extract
2 tablespoons oat milk or other
    milk alternative (page 137)

CARAMEL DONUTS

MAKES ABOUT 8 DONUTS

DONUTS
¼ cup butter or coconut oil, melted
    + more for greasing
1½ cups almond flour
1 teaspoon baking powder
⅓ cup honey or coconut syrup
½ teaspoon almond extract
½ teaspoon vanilla extract
1 teaspoon apple cider vinegar
4 large egg whites

CARAMEL ICING
Caramel Spread (page 131)
2 tablespoons almond
    or other nut butter

ON TOP
Crushed walnuts

Caramel donuts were my favorite when I was a teenager, but my mother rarely let me eat them. Now I have created an excellent substitute that I can munch on without a twinge of guilt!

DONUTS. Preheat the oven to 350°F and position a rack in the center of the oven. Grease a donut pan. Stir the almond flour and baking powder together in a bowl. In another bowl, mix the butter, honey, almond and vanilla extracts, and vinegar. Add the wet ingredients to the dry ingredients and mix well.

In a clean bowl, beat the egg whites until foamy. Fold into the other ingredients carefully. Divide the batter among the donut molds evenly. Bake until the donuts are golden, 15 minutes. Let the donuts cool and remove them from the pan.

ICING. Prepare the caramel spread and add the almond butter. Pour this icing over the donuts. Sprinkle with crushed walnuts and enjoy.

COOKIES, MUFFINS & OTHER SMALL BAKED GOODS

CINNAMON CHOCOLATE DONUTS

A chocolate donut always works, for every moment, every place, and everyone. These lovely chocolate rounds are no exception to the rule.

MAKES ABOUT 8 DONUTS

DONUTS
¼ cup coconut oil + more
    for greasing
¼ cup coconut flour
½ cup almond flour
⅓ cup raw cacao powder
1 teaspoon baking powder
1 teaspoon ground cinnamon
¼ teaspoon sea salt
3 eggs
⅓ cup honey or coconut syrup
1 teaspoon apple cider vinegar
1 teaspoon vanilla extract

Easy Chocolate Icing
    (page 128 or 129)

ON TOP
Crushed walnuts
Coconut flakes

Preheat the oven to 350°F and position a rack in the center of the oven. Grease a donut pan. Mix the flours, cacao powder, baking powder, cinnamon, and salt in a bowl. Separate the egg yolks and whites into two clean bowls. To the bowl with the yolks, add the honey, apple cider vinegar, vanilla extract, and ¼ cup coconut oil. Beat together. Pour this mixture in with the dry ingredients. Whisk the egg whites until foamy and add those in with the rest. Divide evenly among the donut molds. Bake until golden, 10–15 minutes. Let the donuts cool and remove them from the pan.

Prepare the icing and pour over the donuts. Sprinkle crushed walnuts and coconut flakes on top, then serve.

These vegan vanilla donuts are a beautiful and dainty snack. Perfect for a Sunday treat or the moment before a nap.

CARDAMOM VANILLA DONUTS

Preheat the oven to 350°F and position a rack in the center of the oven. Grease a donut pan. Prepare the "flaxseed egg" by mixing the flaxseeds and water and letting the mixture sit for 5–10 minutes.

In a bowl, stir together the flours, baking powder, psyllium husk powder, and cardamom. Mash the banana in another bowl and add in rice milk, "flaxseed egg," and melted butter. Sweeten with the vanilla stevia. Add the dry ingredients from the other bowl and mix into a batter. Spoon the batter into the donut pan, dividing evenly, and bake until slightly golden, about 25 minutes. Remove from the oven and let cool. Prepare the icing.

ICING. Melt the cacao butter and coconut oil in the top of a double boiler. Add the sweetener and rice milk. Transfer the bowl to an ice-water bath and stir with a spoon until the mixture starts to thicken. You can also pop the mixture in the fridge to set, but make sure not to keep it there too long, or it will be too stiff. Pour the icing over the cooled donuts and sprinkle with puffed rice and/or dust with rice flour using a sieve. Serve and enjoy.

MAKES ABOUT 8 DONUTS

Coconut oil for greasing
1 large "flaxseed egg"
    (3 tablespoons ground flaxseed
    + ⅓ cup warm water)
1 cup rice flour
⅓ cup potato flour
2 teaspoons baking powder
½ teaspoon psyllium husk powder
    or xanthan gum
½ teaspoon ground cardamom
1 ripe banana, peeled
1 cup rice milk
3 tablespoons butter or coconut oil,
    melted
½ teaspoon vanilla stevia,
    or ¼ cup honey + 1 teaspoon
    vanilla extract

WHITE CHOCOLATE VANILLA ICING
½ cup grated cacao butter
3 tablespoons coconut oil
½ teaspoon vanilla stevia or honey
    and vanilla extract
3 tablespoons rice milk or other
    milk alternative (page 137)

ON TOP
Puffed rice and/or rice flour

ORANGE FLOWER MARZIPAN BUNS

I highly recommend these marzipan-filled dream rolls to all sticky-bun fanatics. Tip! You can fill these with the Caramel Spread on page 131 in place of the orange marzipan.

MAKES ABOUT 12 BUNS

BUNS

½ cup butter or coconut oil, melted
½ cup coconut sugar
2 large eggs
¼ cup almond milk or other milk alternative (page 137)
1 cup almond flour
1 cup buckwheat flour
1½ tablespoons psyllium husk powder
1 teaspoon baking powder
1 tablespoon ground cardamom
1 teaspoon ground cinnamon
½ teaspoon sea salt

ORANGE MARZIPAN FILLING

Double batch Orange Marzipan (page 23), with liquids doubled twice
2 tablespoons orange-flower water

ON TOP

Beaten egg for brushing (optional)
Coconut sugar
Flaked almonds

BUNS. Preheat the oven to 425°F and position a rack in the center of the oven. Line a muffin pan with paper muffin liners. Beat the butter, coconut sugar, eggs, and almond milk together. In another bowl, mix the flours, psyllium husk powder, and baking powder. Add the cardamom, cinnamon, and salt. Stir the dry ingredients into the wet ingredients little by little. Let the dough rise for about 10 minutes. The dough should be easily moldable, like other bun doughs. Turn your attention to preparing filling.

FILLING. Make the orange marzipan according to the recipe on page 23, doubling the recipe, doubling the liquids again, and adding the orange flower water. (The extra liquids will make the marzipan spreadable.)

Using a rolling pin, roll the dough into a rectangular shape between 2 sheets of parchment paper. If the dough is difficult to work, pop it in the freezer for a bit. This will make handling it easier. Cover the dough with plenty of marzipan filling. Using the parchment paper to help you, roll it up into a large roll. Use a sharp knife to cut crosswise into buns about 1 inch thick. Set the buns into the prepared muffin pans, brush with beaten egg if you wish, and sprinkle with a bit of coconut sugar and flaked almonds. Bake until slightly colored, 10–15 minutes. To keep the buns moist, avoid baking them for too long. The centers should be soft. Remove from the oven, let cool for a bit, serve, and enjoy!

ICE CREAMS
&
SORBETS

LICORICE ICE CREAM

MAKES ABOUT 1 PINT

ICE CREAM BASE
2 large organic eggs
⅓ cup honey or coconut syrup
Whipped Coconut Cream (page 132)

LICORICE SAUCE
⅓ cup dark coconut syrup or honey
2 tablespoons licorice powder

ICE CREAM BASE. In a bowl, beat the eggs and honey until foamy. Prepare the whipped coconut cream and fold into the egg mixture with a rubber spatula.

LICORICE SAUCE. Mix the coconut syrup and licorice powder into a smooth paste.

Pour the ice cream base into an ice cream maker and prepare according to the manufacturer's instructions. At the last moment, pour in the licorice sauce to create stripes in the ice cream. (If you don't have an ice cream maker, pour the mixture into a rimmed dish and freeze for about 3 hours. Stir about every 45 minutes and pour in the licorice sauce halfway through the freezing time.)

I could not shake the thought of licorice ice cream in the summer. After a few tries, I managed to create the treat I wanted. The whole party fell in love with this ice cream when we tested it. It's worth following your dreams!

CARDAMOM PEACH ICE CREAM

MAKES ABOUT 1 PINT

ICE CREAM BASE

3 fresh peaches, peeled and pitted

⅓ cup honey or other sweetener
of your choice, such as
maple syrup

1 teaspoon ground cardamom

1 teaspoon ground cinnamon

2 large egg whites

2 cans (13.5 oz each) full-fat
coconut milk, refrigerated
overnight

WAFFLE CONES (MAKES ABOUT 5)

2 organic egg whites

¼ cup butter or coconut oil, melted
and cooled + more for greasing

½ cup coconut sugar
+ ½ dropperful vanilla stevia

½ cup rice flour

1 teaspoon psyllium husk powder

½ teaspoon pure vanilla powder

Pinch of sea salt

5 tablespoons oat milk or other
milk alternative (page 137)

Coconut oil for greasing

Aluminum foil or cardboard
for the waffle molds

Baked fresh peaches
make a lovely ice cream.
It's especially good when
served in a homemade
waffle cone.

ICE CREAM BASE. Preheat the oven to 400°F. Slice the peaches into a bowl and add the honey, cardamom, and cinnamon. Mix well. Pour this mixture into a baking dish and bake for about 20 minutes. Let cool.

Beat the egg whites until foamy. In another bowl, use the cans of coconut milk to prepare a whipped coconut cream as described on page 132, omitting the additional sweeteners. In a blender, purée the baked peaches. You can blend them smooth or leave in chunks according to your preference. Reserve some of the purée for drizzling over the ice cream. Combine the whipped coconut cream, egg white foam, and peach purée. Pour this ice cream base into an ice cream maker and prepare according to the manufacturer's instructions. (If you don't have an ice cream maker, pour into a rimmed dish and freeze for about 2 hours. Beat the mixture vigorously every 45 minutes using a hand blender or handheld mixer.)

WAFFLE CONES. Put the egg whites in a clean bowl. Add the butter and beat until foamy. Mix the coconut sugar, rice flour, psyllium husk powder, vanilla powder, and salt and add slowly to the butter mixture while beating. Add the oat milk and let sit for about 5 minutes. Prepare cone shapes with foil or cardboard. Warm and grease a waffle iron. Pour a thin layer of the mixture onto the iron, close, and bake for 2–3 minutes. The thinner the layer and the longer you bake, the crisper the waffle cones. Remove the waffle using a spatula and roll it over the cone mold. Let cool, remove from the mold, and place on a wire rack to dry further. Repeat with the remaining batter.

Scoop the ice cream into balls and serve in the cones, drizzled with the reserved peach purée.

MANGO MELON SORBET CAKE

MAKES ABOUT 4 SERVINGS

2 ripe mangos, peeled and pitted
½ honeydew melon or cantaloupe, peeled and seeded
1 ripe banana, peeled

CAKE BASE

½ cup macadamia nuts
½ cup almonds
4 fresh dates, pitted and chopped
Coconut oil for greasing

2 tablespoons honey or coconut syrup
1 tablespoon vanilla extract

HONEY-ROASTED ALMONDS

¼ cup almonds
2 tablespoons honey
2 tablespoons coconut oil

TART PAN SIZE

About 8 x 5 inches

This sorbet cake is my family's favorite summer treat. You can speed up the preparation by blending the frozen fruits, adding the roasted almonds to the mixture, and scooping into balls. Works dandy both ways!

Dice the mango, melon, and banana and freeze them overnight in an airtight container.

CAKE BASE. Grind the nuts in a high-speed blender or food processor. Add the dates and blend into a moldable dough. Grease a high-sided tart pan with a removable base and press the dough into it.

In the blender, gradually add the frozen fruits and purée into a sorbet-like mixture. (Reserve a few spoonfuls of diced mango.) Add the honey and vanilla extract and blend. Spoon this sorbet mixture over the cake base and place the pan in the freezer until solid, about 3 hours.

HONEY-ROASTED ALMONDS. Crush some of the almonds in a mortar and pestle. Combine the honey and coconut oil in a saucepan, add the crushed and whole almonds, and toss and cook lightly until they get a bit of color. Invert the sorbet cake onto a plate and invert it again onto a serving platter. Spoon the roasted almonds over. Serve and enjoy at once!

COOKIE ICE CREAM WITH SALTED PEANUTS

MAKES ABOUT 6 SERVINGS

ICE CREAM

1 cup cashew nuts

1 ripe banana

⅓ cup honey or 1 dropperful
   chocolate stevia

3 tablespoons coconut oil

½ cup full-fat coconut milk
   + more as needed

¼ cup raw cacao powder

COOKIES (MAKES ABOUT 16)

1 cup almond flour

⅓ cup coconut flour

1 tablespoon psyllium husk powder

1 teaspoon baking powder

Pinch of sea salt

⅓ cup honey or coconut syrup

⅓ cup peanut butter
   or other nut butter

⅓ cup coconut oil

2 large eggs

½ teaspoon vanilla extract

1 cup oat milk or other milk
   alternative (page 137)

ON TOP

Ground salted peanuts

ICE CREAM. In a high-speed blender or food processor, combine the cashews with the banana, honey, coconut oil, coconut milk, and cacao powder. Blend into a smooth, thick mixture. Add a splash of coconut milk if necessary to make the mixture smooth. Taste and adjust the flavorings. Pour into the ice cream maker and prepare according to the manufacturer's instructions. (Alternatively, pour into a rimmed dish and freeze for about 3–4 hours. Stir every 45 minutes to break up the ice crystals and to keep the ice cream fluffy.) Meanwhile, it's time to prepare the cookies.

COOKIES. Preheat the oven to 350°F and line a baking sheet with parchment paper. Mix the flours, psyllium husk powder, baking powder, and salt in a bowl. Melt the honey, peanut butter, and coconut oil in the top of a double boiler. Pour this mixture into another bowl and add the eggs and vanilla extract. Beat to a fluffy mixture. Keep mixing and add the dry ingredients. Add the oat milk and mix into a dough.

Take a tablespoonful of dough at a time, roll into a ball, and place on the prepared baking sheet. Using wet hands, press the balls into flat cookies. Bake for about 12 minutes. Transfer the cookies to a wire rack and let cool completely.

ASSEMBLY. Scoop the ice cream into small balls and press each between 2 cookies. Roll the sides of the ice cream cookies in the salted peanuts. Serve at once, or keep in the freezer until you do.

If you love the combination of sweet and salty, and nut butter, these are for you. The superb pairing of the soft-textured cookies with chocolate ice cream rolled in salted peanuts is one you won't forget. Freeze the leftover cookies for later use.

These delicious handcrafted chocolate ice pops are easy to make in Popsicle molds. You can prepare the icing below, or simply use a melted raw chocolate bar with some crushed nuts thrown in.

ICE CREAM. Combine the bananas, nut butter, and almonds in a high-speed blender or food processor and blend, adding just enough of the water to create a smooth, thick mixture. (Too much water will make the ice cream crystallize.) Add the cacao nibs, honey, and vanilla powder. Pulse to mix, leaving the cacao nibs in pieces. Pour into ice pop molds and freeze for a few hours. Just before you are ready to serve, prepare the icing.

ICING. Melt the cacao butter and coconut oil in the top of a double boiler. Add the cacao powder, honey, and salt. Bring the ice pops from the freezer and, using a spoon, coat them with the chocolate icing. Sprinkle the crushed nuts on top, if you wish. Serve immediately, or keep in the freezer on a plate.

ARTISANAL DREAMSICLES

MAKES ABOUT 4 SERVINGS

ICE CREAM
2 ripe bananas, peeled and
    sliced
2 heaping tablespoons nut
    butter
¼ cup almonds
5 tablespoons water
2 tablespoons raw cacao
    nibs
1 tablespoon honey or
    coconut syrup
½ teaspoon vanilla powder

CHOCOLATE ICING
⅓ cup grated raw cacao
    butter
2 tablespoons coconut oil
¼ cup raw cacao powder
1 tablespoon honey or
    coconut syrup
Small pinch of sea salt

ON TOP
Crushed nuts (optional)

Combine the 1 cup cherries, coconut oil, honey, and vanilla extract in a high-speed blender or food processor and mix. Add the hemp seeds, cacao powder, and, if necessary to get a smooth mixture, a splash of water. With a spoon, stir in the ⅓ cup chopped cherries and the raw chocolate.

Pour the mixture into an ice cream maker and prepare the ice cream according to the manufacturer's instructions. (If you don't have an ice cream maker, pour the mixture into a rimmed dish and freeze for a few hours. Mix well every 45 minutes to make sure the ice cream stays fluffy.)

When the ice cream is ready, scoop into balls, serve, and enjoy!

This sinfully delicious cherry-studded chocolate ice cream contains hemp seeds as a surprise healthful ingredient, though you can taste only the cherries and chocolate.

CHERRY-CHOCOLATE ICE CREAM

MAKES ABOUT 1 PINT

1 cup pitted whole fresh cherries + ⅓ cup chopped cherries
2 tablespoons coconut oil, melted
⅓ cup honey or coconut sugar
1 teaspoon vanilla extract
½ cup hemp seeds
⅓ cup raw cacao powder
Water or milk alternative (page 137), as needed
¼ cup (2 oz) ground raw chocolate, purchased or homemade (see Basic Chocolate, page 12)

ICE CREAMS & SORBETS

ESKIMO SQUARES

MAKES ABOUT 6 SERVINGS

ICE CREAM

½ cup cashew nuts, soaked for
    1 hour
½ cup macadamia nuts
½ cup oat milk or other milk
    alternative (page 137)
⅓ cup coconut oil, melted
2 tablespoons honey
1 tablespoon vanilla extract
8 drops stevia, or as needed

Double batch Easy Chocolate Icing
    (page 128 or 129)

CONTAINER SIZE

About 5 x 10 inches

Simple pleasures like vanilla ice cream are unbeatable. This ice cream recipe is a thank-you for two of the basic ingredients of life: vanilla ice cream and chocolate.

ICE CREAM. Drain and rinse the soaked nuts and combine them in a high-speed blender or food processor with the oat milk. Blend into a smooth mixture. Add the coconut oil, honey, vanilla extract, and stevia. Blend until smooth. Line a high-sided dish with plastic wrap or parchment paper, letting it drape over the sides, and pour the mixture in. Freeze until solid, about 3 hours. Bring the dish out and cut the ice cream into squares. Return the squares to the freezer.

Prepare a double batch of an easy chocolate icing.

Bring the squares out of the freezer and dip the pieces one at a time into the chocolate icing. You can also coat the squares with the chocolate using a spoon. Place on a serving plate lined with parchment paper and keep in the freezer until serving.

TIP! If you want to keep the color of the ice cream filling white, be sure to use light honey and stevia as sweeteners.

STRAWBERRY ROSE ICE CREAM

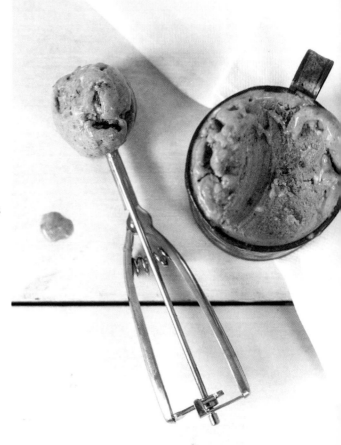

MAKES ABOUT 1 PINT

ICE CREAM
1½ cups fresh or frozen strawberries
1 ripe banana, peeled and sliced
1 cup full-fat coconut milk
½ teaspoon pure vanilla powder
1 teaspoon rose extract
3 large egg whites

CHOCOLATE ICING
4 ounces unsweetened dark or
    raw chocolate, purchased or
    homemade, or ½ cup Basic
    Chocolate (page 12)

Set about ¼ cup of the strawberries aside. Pour the rest of them into a blender. Add the banana, coconut milk, vanilla powder, and rose extract and blend to a smooth mixture.

Put the egg whites in a bowl and beat to stiff, glossy peaks. Fold in the strawberry mixture. Cut the rest of the strawberries into the bowl with kitchen scissors and fold in. Taste and adjust the sweetness if you like. Use the mixture to make ice cream according to your ice cream makers' instructions. Alternatively, you can place the bowl in the freezer for a few hours, stirring it every 30–45 minutes.

Enjoy as is, or make an icing. In the top of a double boiler, melt the raw or unsweetened dark chocolate, or use the Basic Chocolate. Scoop the ice cream into balls and dip them into the melted chocolate. The chocolate will set over the frozen ice cream immediately. Serve and enjoy!

TIP! Make a vegan version by replacing the egg whites with ⅓ cup macadamia nuts and 2 tablespoons of melted coconut oil.

Strawberry and rose are
an unbeatable combination.
In ice cream, they go
together beautifully.

Initially, I was going to put this recipe in with the cakes, as this cake does well in the fridge as well. However, it's at its best when frozen and then just slightly thawed.

TIRAMISU ICE CREAM CAKE

MAKES 6 SERVINGS

CREAM FILLING
2 cups macadamia nuts
1½ cups almond milk or other milk alternative (page 137)
⅓ cup honey or coconut syrup
1 tablespoon vanilla extract
½ cup grated cacao butter
⅓ cup coconut oil

CAKE LAYER
1 cup oat flakes
½ cup soft raisins
2 fresh dates, pitted
3 tablespoons coconut oil, melted
¼ cup strong coffee
¼ cup almond liqueur
1 tablespoon raw cacao powder
3 tablespoons honey
1 teaspoon vanilla extract
Pinch of salt

ON TOP
Whipped Coconut Cream (page 132)
Raw cacao powder

CONTAINER SIZE
About 5 x 8 inches

CREAM FILLING. In a high-speed blender or food processor, process the nuts and almond milk until smooth. Add the honey and vanilla extract. Melt the cacao butter and coconut oil in the top of a double boiler. Pour this mixture into the blender with the other ingredients and mix well. Taste and adjust the sweetness or flavorings if you wish. Pour half of the mixture into a high-sided rectangular dish and set in the freezer for about 30 minutes. Place the rest in a bowl and reserve. Prepare the cake layer.

CAKE LAYER. In a blender, process the oat flakes, raisins, dates, coconut oil, coffee, and liqueur into a dough. Add the cacao powder, honey, vanilla extract, and salt. Mix well. Taste and adjust the flavorings.

When the cream filling has set a bit, bring the dish from the freezer and spoon half of the cake layer on top. Pour the reserved cream filling over the cake layer. Return to the freezer until the surface has set. Bring out and spoon the remainder of the cake layer on top and return to the freezer for a few hours.

Make the whipped coconut cream. Take the dish out of the freezer and invert to unmold the cake onto a baking sheet. Fill a piping bag with the whipped coconut cream and decorate the cake. Dust with cacao powder. Serve right away, or keep in the freezer until serving.

GARNISHES,
JAMS
&
SPREADS

Put the coconut flakes in a high-speed blender or food processor and grind them on medium speed to the consistency of a flour. Keep the machine on until the mixture starts to become sticky and grainy. If needed, use a rubber spatula to scrape the mixture from the sides of the bowl to the center. When the mixture starts to resemble butter, turn the machine on full speed to make the mixture as smooth as possible. Making coconut butter takes between 1–5 minutes, depending on your machine's power. Add the vanilla powder and mix lightly. Use a glass jar with a tightly closing lid to store the coconut butter. It will keep for several weeks at room temperature. Don't keep it in the fridge, because this will make it hard to spread. (You can use a double boiler to soften hardened coconut butter.)

VANILLA COCONUT BUTTER

MAKES ABOUT 1 CUP

2 cups coconut flakes
1 teaspoon pure vanilla powder

This coconut butter can work in baking, as a spread, or as an icing for confections. It's a bit sweet, so you may want to cut down on the other sweeteners.

Nut and almond butters are great to use as a spread, in baked goods, as icing, or however you like. The almonds can be replaced with different nuts, and the chocolate can be left out.

CHOCOLATE ALMOND BUTTER

MAKES ABOUT 1 CUP

1½ cups blanched almonds
1 tablespoon almond oil (optional)
3 tablespoons raw cacao powder
1 tablespoon coconut oil, melted
3 tablespoons honey or coconut
   syrup
Pinch of sea salt

Put the almonds in a high-speed blender or food processor. Grind into a fine meal and keep mixing until the almond meal starts to take on a waxlike appearance. Add a bit of almond oil, if needed; with a powerful blender you can make almond butter with no added oil. Keep blending until the mixture becomes almond butter. The process will take about 15 minutes. Add the cacao powder, coconut oil, honey, and salt. Mix well.

2 × EASY CHOCOLATE ICING

DATE CHOCOLATE ICING

MAKES ABOUT ½ CUP

½ cup fresh dates, pitted
⅓ cup coconut oil, melted
⅓ cup raw cacao powder
⅓ cup water, or as needed

In a blender, process the dates and melted coconut oil until smooth. Add the cacao powder and keep the machine running, adding water in small amounts until you get the thickness you want. Use as a filling or as an icing.

TIP! The only requirement for success is that the dates be soft and juicy. Medjool dates are the best. If the dates feel dry, soak them for about an hour.

Choose between these two easy chocolate icings to use as fillings or icings for baked goods.

AVOCADO CHOCOLATE ICING

MAKES ABOUT 1 CUP

1 tablespoon ground raw cacao butter
2 tablespoons coconut oil
⅓ cup honey
⅓ cup raw cacao powder
2 ripe avocadoes, halved and pitted

Melt the cacao butter in the top of a double boiler with the coconut oil and honey. Add the cacao powder. Chop and scoop the avocados into a blender and add the melted cacao mixture. Mix until smooth.

GARNISHES, JAMS & SPREADS

CARAMEL SPREAD

MAKES ABOUT 1 CUP

15–20 fresh dates
2 tablespoons coconut oil
½ teaspoon vanilla extract
½ teaspoon sea salt
1–5 tablespoons water

Use this caramel sauce as an icing, a filling, an ice cream topping, a dip, or a spread. Soft Medjool dates are the best for this recipe.

Pit the dates. If you want the caramel to be very soft, and you don't know how powerful your blender is, also remove the peels. (Peeling fresh dates is easy under running water.) Combine the dates and coconut oil in the blender and purée. Add the vanilla extract and salt and mix again. Add in enough water to make the mixture a smooth and runny purée. Spoon the caramel sauce into a glass jar with a tightly closing lid. Keep in the fridge.

WHIPPED COCONUT CREAM

MAKES ABOUT 2 CUPS

2 cans (13.5 oz each) full-fat
 coconut milk, refrigerated
 overnight
1–2 tablespoons honey or coconut
 syrup
½ teaspoon pure vanilla powder

This is the perfect replacement for the traditional whipped cream used in baked goods and icings. Note that coconut milk brands differ: some make thick whipped cream easily, some not so well. Try different brands until you find your favorite!

Open the 2 cans of coconut milk from the bottom and drain out the clear liquid. (Reserve this liquid for another use, such as a smoothie.) Spoon the thick coconut cream from the cans into a bowl. Beat with an electric mixer until the mixture becomes thick. Lift the mixer regularly while mixing to aerate the cream and make it fluffy. Add the honey and vanilla powder. Refrigerate if the whipped coconut cream turns too runny. Use as icing or for decorating as you would regular whipped cream.

TIP! When you're buying coconut milk, give the can a shake. If you hear splashing, don't buy that can. If you hear a heavy slush, drop it in your basket.

PEANUT BUTTER SPREAD

MAKES ABOUT 1 CUP

½ cup butter or coconut oil
½ cup unsweetened peanut butter
4 tablespoons honey or coconut
   syrup
1 tablespoon vanilla extract
3 tablespoons oat milk (page 137)

In a saucepan, combine the butter, peanut butter, and honey and melt to a smooth mixture over medium heat. Stir in the vanilla extract and oat milk. Mix well. Remove the pan from the heat and pour the mixture into a bowl. Place in the fridge for about 15 minutes. Take the bowl out of the fridge and beat with an mixer into a fluffy, light spread.

This spread is great to use as a filling or topping for baked goods and cakes. Vegans can replace the butter with coconut oil and the honey with coconut syrup. The mixture will turn quite solid in the fridge.

Who needs cow's milk when the plant-based alternatives can be made easily and cheaply? Try different ingredients, and you'll find your favorite. Milk alternatives are great to cook with and drink!

DAIRY-FREE MILK ALTERNATIVES

ALMOND MILK

MAKES ABOUT 2 CUPS

1 cup almonds (soaked overnight in
    water to cover, if you like)
2 cups water
2 fresh dates, pitted and coarsely
    chopped
½ teaspoon pure vanilla powder

Process the almonds soaked or not, water, and dates in a blender to a smooth consistency. Strain out the fibers with a colander lined in cheesecloth to get the milk smooth. Season with the vanilla powder. Store in an airtight bottle or jar in the fridge. Drink within 4–5 days. Shake before using.

OAT MILK

MAKES ABOUT 2 CUPS

1 cup oat flakes
2 cups water, or as needed
2 tablespoons honey
½ teaspoon ground cinnamon
½ teaspoon pure vanilla powder
¼ teaspoon sea salt

Rinse the oat flakes and soak them for about 30 minutes. Rinse again. Combine with the 2 cups water in a blender. You can add more water if you'd like the milk to be thinner. Blend at full speed for about 15 seconds. Strain the milk and save the oat solids for later baking. Rinse the blender and pour the milk back in. Blend again and strain. You can strain the milk as many times as you'd like. Usually 3 times is enough to make the milk smooth. Add the honey, cinnamon (if using), vanilla powder, and salt during the last round of mixing. Store in an airtight bottle or jar in the fridge. Drink within 4–5 days. Shake before using.

SESAME MILK

MAKES ABOUT 2 CUPS

1 cup unhulled sesame seeds
4 fresh dates, pitted
2 cups water
½ teaspoon pure vanilla powder
¼ teaspoon sea salt

Soak the sesame seeds for about 6 hours or overnight. Soak the dates in a separate container. Drain and rinse the sesame seeds. Add the water, drained sesame seeds, and dates to a blender. Blend at full speed for about 30 seconds. Strain. Add the vanilla and salt and mix. Store in an airtight bottle or jar in the fridge. Drink within 4–5 days. Shake before using.

DAIRY-FREE YOGURTS

Delicate milk-free yogurts are easy to
create using coconut or almonds.

COCONUT YOGURT

MAKES ABOUT 1 CUP

1 can full-fat coconut milk,
   refrigerated overnight
2 probiotic capsules
1–2 tablespoons honey
½ teaspoon pure vanilla powder

Sterilize a glass jar in boiling water (or by washing it in
a dishwasher). Dry the glass carefully. Scrape the white
thick layer of coconut cream from the coconut milk can
into the jar and add as much coconut milk from the can as
needed to achieve a consistency you like. Open 2 probiotic
capsules, pour the powder into the jar, and mix with
a spoon. Add the honey. Place a folded cheesecloth or
other clean cloth over the jar opening and secure it with a
rubber band. Turn on your oven light, but do not turn the
oven on. Place the jar in the oven and let stand overnight.
The next day, stir in the vanilla and chill the yogurt in
the fridge.

ALMOND YOGURT

MAKES ABOUT 1½ CUPS

1 cup almonds, soaked for 1 hour
1 cup oat milk or other milk
   alternative (page 137)
2 probiotic capsules
1–2 tablespoons honey
½ teaspoon pure vanilla powder

Sterilize a glass jar in a boiling water (or by washing it in
a dishwasher). Dry the glass carefully. Drain and rinse the
soaked almonds and place them in a blender. Add the oat
milk and blend as smooth as possible. Pour this mixture
into the jar. Open 2 probiotic capsules, pour the powder
into the jar, and mix with a spoon. Stir in the honey. Place
a folded cheesecloth or other clean cloth over the jar
opening and secure it with a rubber band. Turn on your
oven light, but do not turn the oven on. Place the jar in
the oven and let stand overnight. The next day, stir in the
vanilla and chill the yogurt in the fridge.

TIP! You can boost the fermentation process by warming
the mixture a bit before adding the probiotic powder.
Store the yogurt in a fridge and use within 1 week. The
yogurt will get thicker the longer you store it.

CHIA JAMS

When chia seeds meet water, they naturally form a gel. You can take advantage of this to create tasty jams. Try different berries and fruits alone or in combos. You can also make jam with flaxseeds, which react with water the same way.

ROSE RASPBERRY JAM

MAKES ABOUT 1 CUP

1 cup fresh or frozen raspberries
⅓ cup honey
Small handful organic rose petals, or 2 teaspoons rose extract
¼ cup chia seeds or ground flaxseed, or as needed

Combine the raspberries, honey, and rose petals or extract in a blender. Purée until smooth or leave in some chunks. Spoon into an airtight glass jar and mix in enough chia seeds to give a consistency you like. Let set in the fridge overnight. Use as a jam, filling, or however you want. Keep in the fridge and use within a week.

TIP! Flaxseeds are slightly harder than chia seeds, so I grind them before using them to make jam.

PEACH LAVENDER JAM

MAKES ABOUT 1 CUP

¼ cup water
2 tablespoons dried lavender
    flowers
3 large peaches, pitted
⅓ cup honey
¼ cup chia seeds or ground
    flaxseed

Boil the water and pour it over
the lavender flowers. Let steep for
about 20 minutes, then strain out
the flowers, reserving the lavender
water. Chop the peaches and place
in a blender. Add the lavender water
and honey. Blend. Pour into a glass
jar with an airtight lid. Stir in the chia
seeds. Let set for at least 30 minutes,
or overnight. Keep in the fridge and
use within a week.

INDEX

THANKS

Alva and Finn—my lovely, lovely family. Mom and Dad for always supporting me no matter what I'm doing. Risto Vauras, Aleksi Koskinen, and Iiro Muttilainen for teaching me about photography and photo editing. Annukka Saukkonen for this beautiful layout. My friends Maiju, Lotta, Noora, and everyone who has been my test audience for these recipes. You, dear reader! And all of my amazing followers and supporters who everyday inspire me to continue to develop healthier alternatives for savoring. Find more of my recipes and food photography on vanelja.com and on Instagram at @vanelja.

weldon**owen**

Published in North America by
Weldon Owen, Inc.
1045 Sansome Street, Suite 100
San Francisco, CA 94111
www.weldonowen.com

Weldon Owen is a division of
Bonnier Publishing USA

Copyright © 2015 by Virpi Mikkonen
Photos & Recipes by Virpi Mikkonen
Graphic design: Annukka Alasko
Originally published as *Kiitos hyvää*
First published in Finland in 2015 by Otava

English translation Carol Huebscher Rhoades

Library of Congress Cataloging in Publication data is available.

This edition printed in 2016
10 9 8 7 6 5 4 3 2 1

ISBN 13: 978-1-68188-109-6
ISBN 10: 1-68188-109-8

Printed and bound in China